VALUE-FOCUSED SUPPLY MANAGEMENT

GETTING THE MOST OUT OF THE SUPPLY FUNCTION

THE NAPM PROFESSIONAL DEVELOPMENT SERIES

Michiel R. Leenders
Series Editor

Volume I
VALUE-DRIVEN PURCHASING
Managing the Key Steps in the Acquisition Process
Michiel R. Leenders
Anna E. Flynn

Volume II
MANAGING PURCHASING
Making the Supply Team Work
Kenneth H. Killen
John W. Kamauff

Volume III
VALUE-FOCUSED SUPPLY MANAGEMENT
Getting the Most Out of the Supply Function
Alan R. Raedels

Volume IV
PURCHASING FOR BOTTOM LINE IMPACT
Improving the Organization Through Strategic Procurement
Lisa M. Ellram
Laura M. Birou

VALUE-FOCUSED SUPPLY MANAGEMENT

GETTING THE MOST OUT OF THE SUPPLY FUNCTION

Volume III
The NAPM Professional Development Series

Alan R. Raedels, Ph.D., C.P.M.
School of Business Administration
Portland State University

Tempe, Arizona

Chicago • London • Singapore

Senior sponsoring editor: *Cynthia A. Zigmund*
Project editor: *Ethel Shiell/Montgomery Media*
Production manager: *Bob Lange*
Art coordinator: *Montgomery Media*
Compositor: *Montgomery Media*
Typeface: *11/13 Times Roman*
Printer: Book Press

Library of Congress Cataloging-in-Publication Data

Raedels, Alan R.
   Value-focused supply management: getting the most out of the
supply function/Alan R. Raedels.
      p. cm.—(The NAPM professional development series; v. 3)
   Includes bibliographical references and index.
   ISBN 0-7863-0237-2
   1. Business logistics.   2. Delivery of goods—Management.
I. Title. II. Series.
HD38.5.R34   1995
658.7—dc20   94–24842

Printed in the United States of America

3 4 5 6 7 8 9 0 BP 1 0 9 8 7 6

To the one who is closer than a brother
and to my wife, Debbie
and daughters, Sara and Alicia

SERIES OVERVIEW

The fundamental premise for this series of four textbooks is that effective purchasing or supply management can contribute significantly to organizational goals and strategies. This implies that suppliers and the way organizations relate to them are a major determinant of organizational success.

It is recognized that differences do exist between public and private procurement; between purchasing for service organizations, manufacturers, retailers, distributors, and resource processors; between supplying projects, research and development, job shops, and small and large organizations across a host of industries, applications, and needs. Nevertheless, research has shown that there is a large degree of commonality in the acquisition process and its management.

These four textbooks, therefore, cover the common ground of the purchasing field. They are organized in parallel to the National Association of Purchasing Management (NAPM) Certification Program leading to the C.P.M. designation. They are aslo meant to provide a sound, up-to-date perspective on the purchasing field for those who may not be interested in the C.P.M. designation.

The textbooks are organized into four major titles:

1. *Value-Driven Purchasing: Managing the Key Steps In the Acquisition Process*
2. *Managing the Purchasing Function: Making the Supply Team Work*
3. *Value-Focused Supply Management: Getting the Most Out of the Supply Function*
4. *Purchasing for the Bottom Line: Improving the Organization Through Strategic Procurement*

Volume I, *Value-Driven Purchasing: Managing the Key Steps In the Acquisition Process,* focuses on the standard acquisition process and the major steps therein, ranging from need recognition and purchase requests to supplier solicitation and analysis, negotiation, contract execution, implementation, and administration.

Volume II, *Managing the Purchasing Function: Making the Supply Team Work,* focuses on the administrative aspects of the purchasing department, ranging from the development of goals and objectives, maintenance of files and records, and budgeting and performance evaluation. It also deals with the personnel issues of the function including the organization, supervision, and delegation of work, staff performance evaluation, staff training and resulting performance difficulties.

Volume III, *Value-Focused Supply Management: Getting the Most Out of the Supply Function,* begins by identifying material flow activities and decisions, including transportation and packaging requirements, receiving, and interior materials handling. It goes on to cover inventory management and concludes with supply activities such as standardization, cost reduction, and material requirements planning.

Volume IV, *Purchasing for the Bottom Line: Improving the Organization Through Strategic Procurement,* commences with purchasing strategies and forecasting. This is followed by internal and external relationships, computerization, and environmental issues.

It is a unique pleasure to edit a series of textbooks like these with a fine group of authors who are thoroughly familiar with the theory and practice of supply management.

Michiel R. Leenders
Series Editor

PREFACE

This book covers a variety of aspects of the supply process. The focus is not directly on the purchasing process but on the variety of peripheral tasks that support the purchasing process. These areas include inventory control and management, transportation, packaging, receiving, warehouse management, and a number of cost reduction and avoidance activities traditionally coordinated or undertaken by the purchasing function of an organization.

The purpose of this book is to provide the practitioner with an overview of and grounding in the fundamentals of each of these areas. Along with purchasing, these areas are especially important in light of today's competitive environment and the increasing need to actively manage the external supply process. Simultaneously, the text provides information to aid the practitioner in understanding the material that is covered by Module Three of the Certified Purchasing Manager Examination.

ACKNOWLEDGMENTS

I wish to give special thanks to my friend and colleague, Lee Buddress. Without his help, insights, encouragement, and suggestions this work would not have been possible. I would also like to thank Michiel Leenders, series editor and long-time friend and colleague, for his support and help through this process. Lastly, I would like to acknowledge the work of the many authors of the sixth edition of the *C.P.M. Study Guide:* Eugene W. Muller, Don W. Dobler, Harry R. Page, Eberhard Scheuing, Prabir K. Bagchi, Judith A. Baranoski, Joseph L. Cavinato, Michael J. Dunleavy, Donald J. Fesko, Barbara B. Friedman, Henry F. Garcia, Larry C. Giunipero, LeRoy H. Graw, Mary Lu Harding, Earl Hawkes, H. Ervin Lewis, Charles J. McDonald, Jr., Paul K. Moffat, Norbert J. Ore, Merle W. Roberts, and Rene A. Yates. Their work provided the foundation upon which much of this book was built.

Alan R. Raedels, C.P.M.

CONTENTS

Chapter 3: Managing Independent Demand Inventory Systems

Chapter 4: Managing Dependent Demand Systems

SECTION 3: MATERIAL FLOW

Chapter 5: Inbound Logistics

SECTION 4: ANCILLARY SUPPLY FUNCTIONS

Chapter 6: Ancillary Supply Functions

Chapter 7: Managing the Supply Base

SECTION 5: THE FUTURE

Chapter 8: The Future of Supply and Inventory Management

SECTION 1

INTRODUCTION

CHAPTER 1

INTRODUCTION

Xerox, through the use of qualified suppliers, reduced incoming inspections from 85 to 15 percent and reduced defective parts by 73 percent while reducing the supply base from 5,000 to about 400 suppliers.[1]

"Supplier partnerships are critical to the success of Cadillac's Simultaneous Engineering Process. Since 1985, Cadillac has extended the product development responsibilities of suppliers. To minimize variation the supply base was reduced. Not only has this action cut waste and improved the quality of materials supplied, since 1986 it has enabled a 425 percent increase in the number of suppliers shipping on a just-in-time basis."[2]

Schweppes PLC of Stamford, Connecticut purchases about 80 percent of its glass containers from a single source as opposed to the previous sourcing strategy where no one supplier provided over 30 percent.[3]

The examples above illustrate a few of the challenges facing organizations as they compete in a global market. This chapter will first review some of the trends taking place in business and the challenges they bring to purchasing and materials management. The chapter will then highlight some of the contributions purchasing and materials management can make to enhance an organization's competitive position.

---

[1] Marion Mills Steeples, *The Corporate Guide to the Malcolm Baldrige National Quality Award* (Homewood, Ill.: Business One Irwin, 1992), p. 271.

[2] Steeples, p. 275.

[3] Alfred L. Malabre, Jr., "Firm's Inventories Are Remarkably Lean," *The Wall Street Journal*, November 3, 1992.

CURRENT TRENDS IN BUSINESS

Many trends taking place in the marketplace today are affecting an organization's ability to compete. These trends include technological change, shrinking product life cycles, increased competitiveness, small lot production, and increased quality requirements.[4] Each of these has a significant impact on purchasing and materials management.

Technological Change

Organizations today are facing a high rate of technological innovation. Products and services purchased today were not even available five years ago. The traditional rule of thumb in electronics purchasing is that 80 percent of the components purchased today were not available five years ago. Organizations are overwhelmed with the changes in both equipment and products. Ignoring the rapid changes in technology is a sure way to erode competitiveness. To remain competitive, firms must be continually looking to improve their processes and products in light of the available technology. Much of the burden of new process and product identification falls on purchasing and materials management.

Shrinking Product Life Cycles

A second trend is the shrinking of product life cycles. Products that used to have life cycles of five years may be down to two years today. This reduction has led to the need to reduce the length of the product design and development cycle. For example, the automobile industry has seen new product introduction times move from five years to three for firms like Chrysler in pursuit of industry leader Toyota. This means that purchasing must not only be able to bring on board world-class suppliers quickly, but must also track shrinking life cycles of important purchased goods.

Increased Competitiveness

Organizations have also experienced increased competitiveness due in part to the changing global marketplace. The maturing of the European

---

[4]S. E. Stephanou and F. Speigl, *The Manufacturing Challenge: From Concept to Production* (New York: Van Nostrand Reinhold, 1992), pp. 9–10.

Economic Community, the ratification of the North American Free Trade Agreement (NAFTA), and the opening up of Pacific Rim countries are creating worldwide market and sourcing opportunities. This is creating strong cost/price pressures on domestic firms. Purchasing organizations today must be familiar not just with domestic markets, but with international ones, as well.

Reduced Production Lots

Smaller production lots are becoming a way of life in firms today. The principles behind the just-in-time philosophy continue to be implemented in more and more firms, not just because they are the current fad, but for survival. These reduced lot sizes have strong implications for the materials management and supply processes within organizations. Often small lots are desired from the supplier even though this may have the potential to increase inbound transportation costs.

Increased Quality Requirements

Quality has increased in importance and changed in focus. Whereas price often was the primary focus of both buyers and customers, with quality, service, and delivery secondary, quality has now become the dominant criterion.[5] Quality is no longer just conformance to specification but now is more commonly defined as satisfying or even delighting the customer's needs. "In this broader context, the concept of quality affects every organizational area as well as all suppliers."[6]

CHALLENGES TO ORGANIZATION

These trends present a variety of challenges to organizations today and specifically to the management of the supply process. Materials managers now have to deal not only with many more issues than in the past, but also with vastly more complex issues such as zero defect quality, shrinking lead

---

[5] Greg Hutchins, *Purchasing Strategies for Total Quality* (Homewood, Ill.: Business One Irwin, 1992), p. 3.

[6] Hutchins, p. 4.

time requirements, environmental issues, and the need to eliminate various forms of waste. All of these must, of course, be accomplished at lower cost.

Quality

Quality improvement is becoming a way of life in many organizations today. The push for total quality management and just-in-time production has caused many firms to reevaluate their suppliers' quality. For example, if a company spends 70 cents of every sales dollar on purchases and 82 percent of the parts in the final product are from outside sources, if the suppliers' quality is equal to the company's, 82 percent of the defects come from outside.[7] A company cannot improve on the quality delivered by its suppliers except at great expense and effort. The implication for materials managers is that the production of superior quality goods and services requires the use of superior quality suppliers.

Cost

As competition increases, organizations are experiencing continued pressure to reduce costs. As the largest component of costs in many organizations is purchased materials and services, the supply process becomes a major contributor to cost reduction. Therefore, companies are looking to purchasing for ways to reduce or eliminate costs since a competitive strategy that seeks to create a cost advantage must reach into supplier companies if it is to succeed.[8]

Lead Time

The materials manager is facing pressure to improve delivery lead time as well as aid in reducing new product development lead times. Delivery lead time must include supplier lead time as well as internal production lead time. Even with a 99.9 percent on-time delivery performance by suppliers, the remaining 0.1 percent can delay the shipment of finished goods. To avoid delays,

---

[7] E. C. Etienne-Hamilton, *Operations Strategies for Competitive Advantage* (Fort Worth, Tex.: The Dryden Press, 1994), p. 339.

[8] Etienne-Hamilton, p. 338.

Companies tried to deal with the problem by creating huge raw materials and parts inventories, only to find out that higher inventories encouraged vendors to be more unreliable. What started as simply delivery unreliability soon became a quality, cost, delivery, and inventory problem, all perfectly intertwined.[9]

The other dimension of lead time is in product development. Lack of involvement of suppliers in the design process can result in delays in bringing a product to market because of design problems, lack of adequate supplies, and lack of time for suppliers to retool and develop the necessary processes. For example, in the automotive industry suppliers were brought in near the end of the product design and development cycle and told to make the specified item at the target cost. Chrysler used to involve suppliers about a year and one-half before production was scheduled to begin. Today, suppliers are involved from the beginning of product development, which is three years before model introduction.

Elimination of Waste

The increased attention to continuous improvement means purchasing and materials managers need to look for ways to eliminate waste in the supply process. The seven wastes are the waste of overproduction, waiting, transportation, unnecessary processing, stocks, motion, and defective products.[10] Each of these areas has a materials management component. Overproduction and waiting can be partially addressed through scheduling, transportation through ordering policies, unnecessary processing through value analysis, stocks through production planning and control, and defective products through improved quality of incoming materials.

Environmental Issues

Along with the increased concern for quality, costs, and lead time, organizations are being forced to become more environmentally conscious. This is beginning to affect materials management in that suppliers must be evaluated on not only their cost and quality but other issues such as

---

[9]Etienne-Hamilton, p. 340.

[10]Robert W. Hall, *Attaining Manufacturing Excellence* (Homewood, Ill.: Dow Jones-Irwin, 1987), p. 26.

recyclability of their materials and packaging and how they deal with hazardous materials. The potential for scarcity of nonrenewable resources has companies searching for substitutes and improving technology. Purchasing and materials management can be proactive by reducing the number of sources, discovering substitute products and processes, and encouraging recycling and reuse of materials. Without early involvement in the design and selection phases of the supply process, purchasing will spend its time acquiring incineration, waste treatment, cleanup, and landfill services.[11]

PURCHASING AND SUPPLY MANAGEMENT CONTRIBUTIONS

With the challenges facing organizations today, how can purchasing and materials management contribute to making organizations more competitive? A recent survey asked top-level purchasing managers to identify the areas where purchasing makes its most significant contributions. Their responses were:

Cost control/reduction of purchased goods	68.3%
Control of supplier quality levels	39.0%
Materials management/production coordination	22.0%
Supplier involvement	19.5%
Improvement of delivery	17.5%[12]

Looking at each of the areas in more detail allows us to see the potential contributions of purchasing and materials management.

Cost Control and Reduction of Purchased Goods

Purchasing can contribute to cost control in several ways. Costs can be reduced through transportation contracting and consolidation. Purchasing is involved with a variety of cost reduction approaches such as value analysis and value engineering, organization-wide buying agreements, long-term contracts, cooperative purchasing, total requirements contracting, and surplus

[11]Michael E. Heberling, "Environmental Purchasing: Separating the Emotions From the Facts," *Logistics —Navigating the Future,* Proceedings of the 78th Annual International Purchasing Conference (Tempe, Ariz.: National Association of Purchasing Management, 1993), p. 77.

[12]Robert M. Monczka and James P. Morgan, "Strategic Sourcing Management," *Purchasing,* July 16, 1992, p. 65.

disposal and recycling efforts. The reduction of purchased goods can be facilitated by improved supplier relationships, including supplier certification, use of standardization programs, and better production planning through the use of material requirements planning and inventory control systems.

Control of Supplier Quality Levels

Supplier quality can be improved through supply base reduction, increased communication with suppliers, early supplier involvement in product and service design, supplier certification, and the use of ISO 9000 standards in supplier qualification and selection. The selection of appropriate transportation modes and proper packaging also can affect quality. Value analysis and value engineering also can be applied to improving the quality of a supplier's products and processes.

Materials Management and Production Coordination

Better coordination between materials management and production can be accomplished by applying material requirements planning (MRP) and manufacturing resource planning (MRP II), by improving inventory accuracy through the use of bar coding and cycle counting, by involving suppliers in product design early, by practicing proper receiving procedures, and by using stores effectively.

Supplier Involvement

Supplier involvement is covered from a number of viewpoints. Topics include the use of early supplier involvement programs in both product and package design, supplier certification, reduction of the supply base, development of recycling agreements, supplier participation on value analysis teams, and application of techniques to improve communication with suppliers such as workshops and symposia.

Improvement of Delivery

Delivery can be improved through supply base reduction, improved communication with suppliers, proper supplier performance measurement, use of MRP and MRP II, more effective use of inbound transportation, supplier certification, and early supplier involvement in product design.

TEXT OVERVIEW

This book is divided into five sections. Sections 2 through 4, which form the heart of the text, are built around Module 3 of the Certified Purchasing Manager Examinations. Each chapter begins with topic coverage followed by a section dealing with purchasing's roles and responsibilities regarding the topic area. A chapter summary highlights key points from the chapter.

Introduction

Chapter 1 sets the stage for the topics to be covered in the remainder of the text. The chapter begins with a presentation of the supply process issues or trends facing organizations today. This is followed by an examination of the challenges these issues present to materials and supply management. The chapter concludes by looking at the contributions purchasing and supply management can make toward meeting those challenges and identifies locations where those contributions are covered in the remainder of the book.

Inventory Management

The inventory management section analyzes the role and costs of inventory and techniques for managing independent and dependent demand inventories. Chapter 2 discusses the functions and costs of inventory, the factors that affect inventory management decisions, measures of inventory performance, techniques for maintaining inventory record accuracy, and purchasing's role in inventory management. Chapter 3 examines both continuous and periodic review inventory systems for independent demand, as well as distribution systems and kanban or just-in-time systems. Chapter 4 reviews dependent demand systems such as material requirements planning (MRP), manufacturing resource planning (MRP II), and distribution requirements planning (DRP).

Material Flow

Chapter 5 in Section 3 on material flow covers a multitude of topics dealing with the flow of materials into the organization. Topics include transportation, packaging requirements, receiving, and warehouse and stores management, concluding with purchasing's responsibilities.

Ancillary Supply Functions

Section 4 on ancillary supply functions deals with topics that do not fit into the buying process or administration of purchasing but are extremely important for competing in today's markets. Chapter 6 deals with standardization, cost reduction and avoidance programs, value analysis and value engineering, and scrap and surplus disposal activities. Chapter 7 covers a number of issues relating to managing the supply base such as sourcing strategies, supplier reduction strategies, methods to improve supplier performance, and supplier certification.

The Future

In Section 5, the final chapter looks to the future of inventory management, logistics, ancillary supply functions, and supply management to highlight both ongoing issues and probable new requirements. The rate at which both purchasing and these supply process activities are changing makes a serious look ahead important.

CHAPTER SUMMARY

This chapter has introduced current trends in business and their effects on materials management and purchasing. Key points are:

- Current trends affecting an organization's ability to compete include technological change, shrinking product life cycles, increased competitiveness, small production lots, and increased quality requirements.

- Materials and purchasing managers are having to deal increasingly with issues relating to quality, cost, lead time, the environment, and the elimination of waste in the supply process.

- Purchasing and supply management can contribute to the organization's competitiveness through cost control, cost reduction, control of supplier quality levels, improved coordination between materials management and production, increased supplier involvement, and improved delivery.

REFERENCES

Etienne-Hamilton, E. C. *Operations Strategies for Competitive Advantage.* Fort Worth, Tex.: The Dryden Press, 1994.

Hall, Robert W. *Attaining Manufacturing Excellence.* Homewood, Ill.: Dow Jones-Irwin, 1987.

Hutchins, Greg. *Purchasing Strategies for Total Quality.* Homewood, Ill.: Business One Irwin, 1992.

Stephanou, S. E., and F. Speigl. *The Manufacturing Challenge: From Concept to Production.* New York: Van Nostrand Reinhold, 1992.

SECTION 2

INVENTORY MANAGEMENT

CHAPTER 2

THE ROLE AND COSTS OF INVENTORY

INTRODUCTION

In response to the recession that hit the paper industry, top management at a paper manufacturer decided to cut as much inventory as possible. That decision, according to the distribution manager, led to a number of damaging outcomes: stockouts, lost business, and a sullied reputation.

[T]his is a classic example of top management making a critical decision with inadequate input. The company's finance leaders, who are paid to see only the bottom line, became the voice of authority. Consequently, top management was reluctant to put up any inventory at all—they saw it as inherently "evil."

The company justified its inventory decision to some incredulous managers by pointing out that the warehouses were still brimming with inventory. However, the problem with this rationalization is that much of the stock has questionable resale value. And a large portion soon will be unsellable, because of normal paper deterioration.[1]

As the above example shows, lack of understanding of the roles and costs of inventory can be extremely expensive. Inventory is one tool in managing the supply process. This chapter will first look at what inventory is, what functions it performs for the firm, and what it costs. Next, the factors that affect inventory management decisions are reviewed, followed

---

[1]"A Cautionary Tale About a Paper Co. That Reduced the Wrong Inventory," *Inventory Reduction Report* 93 (3) (March 1993), p. 12.

by a look at measuring inventory performance and maintaining inventory data accuracy. The chapter concludes with a discussion of managing inventory through managing supply processes and purchasing's role in inventory management. The topics not only will be covered in the traditional view but also will include current thinking as influenced by the just-in-time (JIT) and total quality management (TQM) philosophies.

FORMS OF INVENTORY

Inventory is any material, component, or product that is held for use at a later time. The rationale behind inventory is that it is preferable to have material sitting idle rather than labor or equipment. With this definition in mind, in what forms can inventory be found within the firm? The various forms include:

- *Raw materials* Materials that are purchased for use in producing a product and will be transformed from their original state to a new state. Examples are ore, steel, plastic resin, and flour and consumables such as packaging and catalysts.
- *Components* Materials that are purchased for installation and use in a product but are not transformed. Examples include resistors, fabricated sheet metal cabinets, and radiators.
- *Work-in-process* Materials that are in the midst of the transformation process. Examples are engine assemblies and circuit boards.
- *Finished goods* Completed products that are ready to be shipped or sold to the firm's customers.
- *M.R.O.* Maintenance, repair, and operating supplies used to support the running of the operations. Examples include repair parts, lubricating oils, welding materials, and office supplies.
- *Resale goods* Completed products purchased for resale to the next level in the supply chain. Resale goods inventories are most often found in distributors or wholesalers but can also be found in manufacturers who purchase accessories for inclusion with their product.
- *Other forms* Other forms of inventory include scrap and waste materials, tooling, equipment, and even information.

FUNCTIONS OF INVENTORY

All organizations require some inventory for a variety of reasons. The five major functions of inventory are (1) to meet uncertainty of supply and demand, (2) to anticipate special events, (3) to take advantage of economies of scale, (4) to permit decoupling of operations, and (5) to facilitate transportation of materials from one location to another.

Uncertainty of Supply and Demand

Inventory is maintained because organizations are uncertain about the future demand and supply. Demand uncertainty is not knowing how much of an item or which item will be required by customers during a period of time. A customer can be the firm's customer or an internal operation such as production or maintenance. The primary function of finished good and resale inventories is to handle uncertainty of demand. Uncertainty of supply is not knowing how much or when material will be delivered from a supplier or internal operation. Raw materials, components, and MRO inventories often are kept as protection from supply uncertainty.

Uncertainty of supply and demand can take two forms. The first is quantity uncertainty, not knowing exactly how much will be required or how much will be delivered. Example causes of quantity uncertainty are defects in the materials supplied, varying yield rates in a process, unknown customer plans, or materials ordered by batch that may vary in quantity, such as printing or steel ordered by the melt.

The second form of uncertainty is timing uncertainty. The traditional causes are lead time uncertainty from either suppliers or from internal processes. On the demand side, the firm may have orders for specific quantities from a customer, but the exact timing of the requirement is subject to change.

Inventory kept to handle quantity uncertainty is called buffer or safety stocks. They are set to provide some level of protection or service. The size of the safety stock is determined by the amount of variation per period and the length of time the firm is subject to the risk of a stockout as determined by the lead time for replenishing the material. Determination of safety stocks will be discussed in Chapter 3.

The best approach for handling timing uncertainty is safety lead time. Safety lead time is the amount of time the material is ordered before the normal lead time. If an item is normally ordered with a three-week lead time, using a safety lead time of one week would require that the item be ordered using a four-week lead time. The safety lead time determination is based on the variation in observed delivery times for an item and the probability of delivery within a specified time.

Anticipation

Anticipation inventories are built for special events. Example events are expected material shortages, potential strikes, announced price increases, sales or promotions, and seasonal changes. These inventories are built for a specific purpose. When the cause no longer exists, the inventories should be reduced to normal levels.

Economies of Scale

Economies of scale inventories are increases in stocks caused by management's desire to take advantage of the lower price or cost per unit that can be obtained by ordering or producing larger quantities. The basic tradeoff comes from a lower unit price caused by spreading fixed order or setup costs over a larger unit base or being able to take advantage of a price discount structure through ordering larger quantities at a time versus the increased costs of holding more inventory. An example is ordering a truckload quantity of an item to lower the transportation cost per unit.

Decoupling

Decoupling inventories are inventories held between processes to isolate the operation of one process from another. The objective is to not let the problems in one process directly affect a subsequent process. Decoupling inventories may be built into the process, such as through the use of long conveyors between operations, or may be removable, such as the use of safety stocks. Example uses of decoupling inventories are where a process has high yield variability or the process is a bottleneck operation and materials are held to prevent the bottleneck operation from running out of material.

Transportation

Transportation or pipeline inventories are held to facilitate the moving of material from one location to another. The move could be internal to a facility or between facilities. An example is the oil in transit between the North Slope of Alaska, and Valdez, Alaska, in the Alaskan pipeline. It is inventory that is owned but is not available for use because it is in transit. An internal transportation example is the holding of material until a pallet is filled so it can be moved using a lift truck.

MANAGING INVENTORY BY MANAGING SUPPLY PROCESSES

The functions of inventory do not go away by adopting different business approaches such as total quality management or just-in-time. One can attempt to manage uncertainty by the use of safety stocks, but the only way to truly reduce uncertainty inventory is to reduce the uncertainty in the supply process. This means identifying whether the uncertainty is in quantity or timing. To reduce quantity uncertainty, undertake programs designed to improve incoming defect levels, reduce quantity variations from suppliers, and reduce variation and increase yield rates in internal processes. On the demand side, reducing the replenishment lead time reduces the exposure to risk thereby reducing the quantity of safety stocks needed. To reduce lead time variation, undertake programs aimed at shortening process lead times as well as ensuring on-time delivery. These approaches have strong implications for the choice and management of the supplier base.

Economies of scale inventories are reduced by managing the costs that determine the order quantities. Reducing setup and order costs by reducing setup times and eliminating the waste in the order process will reduce the quantities required to be ordered. Also purchasing strategies such as system contracts, annual contracts, and supplier partnering can allow the firm to gain the pricing advantages of large quantities while ordering only for current needs.

Reduction of decoupling inventories is accomplished through process improvement activities. Focusing on ways to reduce the process variation or finding alternate methods for producing the product both can help reduce the need for decoupling inventories.

Transportation inventories are reduced by a variety of means. Shortening the supply line through using local suppliers is one way. Others include sharing inbound freight with several local companies or having several suppliers share the same inbound shipment. Shortening the pipeline reduces inventories such as raw materials and components. For example, Xerox established a regular route with 25 suppliers within a 40-mile radius of its Rochester, New York, plant covering about 110 items. A Xerox truck visits each supplier daily and picks up a day's worth of the items each supplier provides. The quantities are the same each day for a fixed production period.[2]

The key to improving inventory performance is understanding that inventories are effectively reduced only by improving the firm's processes. Inventory is the result of processes and their control systems. Better control can reduce inventory levels, but the major gains can be made only through changing the processes. *You don't manage inventory, you manage processes.*

COSTS OF INVENTORY

Inventory is not free. Four major categories of costs are associated with having inventory on hand: carrying, ordering, stockout, and cost of the product itself. Although inventory traditionally is considered an asset, inventory may be thought of as a liability since it only incurs costs.

When trying to evaluate the costs of inventory, the decision maker needs to consider all the relevant costs associated with each category. A relevant cost is one that will change in the short term as the level of inventory or the number of orders changes. The acid test is whether money will be saved if the inventory is reduced, the number of orders is reduced, or the number of stockouts is reduced. This concept is based on the assumption that one purchase order results in one order receipt. Application of the newer materials management strategies may result in one purchase order with multiple receipts over time.

Carrying Costs

Carrying costs, also called holding costs, are the costs associated with having inventory available. Carrying costs can be divided into four components: finance costs, ownership costs, risk costs, and overhead costs.

---

[2]Edward J. Hay, *The Just-In-Time Breakthrough* (New York: John Wiley and Sons, 1988), p. 123.

Finance Costs

Finance costs recognize that capital is required to finance the inventory. One approach is to use the interest rate associated with the source of the funds. This is usually the firm's short-term borrowing rate. A second approach is to use the opportunity cost associated with the rate of return required of investments elsewhere in the firm. For example, if the interest rate for short-term borrowing was 12 percent but the firm required all investments to return at least 18 percent, the opportunity cost approach would use 18 percent as the financing cost while the interest rate approach would use 12 percent. The effect is that the economic order quantity would be 22 percent lower using the higher financing cost in this example.

Ownership Costs

Ownership costs are those associated with having material on hand. The two main components are insurance and taxes. Insurance costs are the premiums paid for fire and theft protection. Taxes are property taxes paid based on the value of the inventory at a particular point in time.

Risk Costs

Risk costs are associated with having material on hand for some period of time. Examples are obsolescence, theft, damage, and shrinkage. Obsolescence costs are the costs for material or product inventories that are no longer useful to the firm. They could be technologically obsolete products or components that have been replaced with a different part. The obsolescence rate may also be a function of the inventory turnover. For example, one electronics firm estimated their obsolescence rate at 4 percent when their inventory level was at 2.5 turns per year but only 2 percent at 6 turns per year. Theft and damage are the losses due to product being stolen or unusable. Shrinkage has different meanings in different industries. In retail, shrinkage may mean items lost by theft or improper record keeping. In agricultural products, shrinkage can mean the change in the weight of the product due to moisture loss. For example, if 100 cantaloupes were bought today each weighing 1 pound and then were sold over the next three days, the sales records might show sales for only 96 pounds even though all 100 cantaloupe were sold. The difference of 4 pounds is shrinkage.

Overhead Costs

Overhead costs are costs associated with space, handling, and control. Space costs that may be relevant are warehouse space (especially if the charges are incurred based on the space occupied or volume of business such as in a public warehouse), security for a bonded warehouse, or utilities for a cold storage facility. Handling costs are those associated with the warehouse personnel, and control costs are those associated with operating and maintaining the materials control system. If these costs vary as the inventory level changes, they should be considered.

My own surveys of purchasing professionals have shown that carrying cost, measured as a percent of the product's value, ranges from 24 to 36 percent per year per unit. Lambert and Stock make the point that these magic numbers have been around for decades, citing 13 different sources, in spite of radical changes in costs and interest rates.[3] It is important that each firm estimate its own costs of carrying inventory so that the firm can truly understand how expensive inventory really is. It might even be appropriate to have different carrying costs for different classes or families of items. For example, low-volume or low-value items may have relatively low obsolescence costs and financing costs may be better approximated by the short-term interest rate. High-volume or high-value items, such as finished goods, may have higher obsolescence rates, and finance costs should be based on opportunity costs, since the building of finished goods inventory should be a conscious strategy decision to improve the firm's competitive position.

Ordering Costs

Ordering costs include both the costs of placing an order, either internally or externally, and the costs associated with producing the order, often called setup costs.

Ordering costs are incurred in the process of identifying suppliers and placing replenishment orders. Example costs include forms costs, telephone charges, computer time, postage, direct clerical labor, and the costs of the purchasing professionals. Setup related costs include direct setup labor, setup scrap, lost productivity, and tooling costs.

There is some discussion regarding whether the cost of the purchasing professionals should be included in the ordering costs since their costs are fixed in the short term. If the cost of the purchasing professionals is

---

[3] Douglas M. Lambert and James R. Stock. *Strategic Logistics Management,* 3rd ed. (Homewood, Ill.: Irwin, 1993), p. 366.

omitted, is the cost of acquiring materials understated? The rationale for including this cost is that if buyers kept track, time could be allocated to each order. On the other hand, since this is a fixed cost, an increase in the volume of orders will have very little effect, especially if the increase consists of order releases. Is this a marginal decision or a total cost decision? Traditionally, replenishment decisions are viewed as marginal cost decisions. Are we overcharging the small order and undercharging the large contract? Each counts as one order, but they do not reflect equal effort by purchasing. One approach to this problem is to develop a cost for each item or family of items. Therefore, items that are produced internally would have a cost based on the relevant setup activities; production materials purchases would reflect the cost of order releases; and MRO supplies might reflect the purchase transaction cost from specification to delivery.

Firms often estimate that ordering costs range between $40 and $60 per order. Today, many firms are beginning to believe that the costs really are closer to $150 per order when the accounts payable function and receiving are included in the process. Although this is insignificant on a multimillion dollar order, probably 80 percent of all purchase orders are for under $500. For example, the 1993 Center for Advanced Purchasing Studies (CAPS) benchmark study for the telecommunications services industry shows an average cost per purchase order of $90.82 based on the cost of operating the purchasing department alone.[4]

Stockout Costs

Stockout costs are the costs of not having the proper material on hand when it is needed. In general, stockout costs are among the hardest to measure as many firms do not regularly collect such data.

Stockout costs can be divided into several categories—extra production costs, extra transportation costs, extra clerical costs, and lost customer and revenue costs. Extra production costs include pay for workers who are idle because of a lack of material; extra setup costs, including direct labor and waste; overtime; and lost productivity. Extra transportation costs include premium freight charges such as air freight charges or

---

[4] Debra S. Seaman and Michael T. Haskell, *Purchasing Performance Benchmarks for the U.S. Telecommunications Services Industry* (Tempe, Ariz.: Center for Advanced Purchasing Studies, 1993).

higher (less-than-truckload or less-than-carload) rates, or demurrage or detention charges caused by missing the scheduled ship date. Extra clerical costs include additional paperwork for back orders, order splits, or partial shipments. On the more esoteric side are costs such as lost revenue, lost profit margin, or a lost customer. Although these may be real, measuring them is a difficult task at best. This does not mean they are not relevant.

Product Costs

Product costs are those associated with each item, including transportation costs and price discounts. The product cost is part of the total cost of inventory and will affect the total carrying cost, as total carrying cost is based on the carrying costs as a percentage of product cost. In the effort to manage inventory effectively, it is vital to understand what the relevant costs of inventory are.

FACTORS AFFECTING INVENTORY MANAGEMENT DECISIONS

The level of inventory within the firm is a strategic decision; the control of that inventory is an operational activity. A variety of factors affect inventory decisions, such as the value, demand pattern, availability, customer requirements, source, material state, and performance measures used to evaluate the manager's performance.

Value

The value of an item depends on its cost, volume, relationship with other items, and criticality to the continued operation of the firm. Some items may be low cost but the large volume makes the total cost significant. Another item may have high value because it is coupled with another item to create a set. The greater the value of an item, the more closely it needs to be controlled.

Demand Pattern

The demand pattern for an item has at least two dimensions. The first dimension is whether demand for the items to be controlled is dependent or independent. Independent demand items are items for which the demand is independent of the demand for any other item. Normally this refers to finished goods items. Examples are television sets, office supplies, or MRO items. Dependent demand items are those whose demand is triggered by the demand for another item or items. An example is the components that go into a television set. In manufacturing, probably 80 to 90 percent of production items are dependent; in wholesale or retail, 90 percent or more of the items are probably independent. The primary issues with independent demand items are forecasts of usage and replenishment times. Dependent items can be planned more accurately, as their demand is dependent on the master production schedule. Some items, such as spare parts, may have both dependent and independent demand.

The second dimension to the demand pattern is that of seasonality. An item with strong seasonality needs a system that allows alternate ordering quantities and keeps track of the seasonality from year to year. The seasonality of an item also interacts with the capacity of the firm, possibly causing the firm to build inventory during nonpeak periods to give adequate material or product availability during peak periods.

Availability

A third factor affecting inventory management is the availability of an item. Availability can be classified as abundance, production-based scarcity, or natural scarcity. Items in abundant supply may not require the firm to keep a large supply on hand as they can be obtained easily. The inventory strategy would focus on managing the supply base to keep product costs and inventories as low as possible.

Production-based scarcity occurs when the raw materials may be abundant but the availability of the item itself is limited by a lack of manufacturing capacity within the industry. An example is silicon wafers for integrated circuits. The raw materials are plentiful in nature, but the availability of product is limited by the capacity of the industry. The inventory strategy would include actively building relations with suppliers, keeping a close eye on lead times, and communicating with suppliers about the firm's future needs.

Natural scarcity occurs when an item, usually a raw material, is limited by its availability in nature, for example chromium, which is found in only a few regions in the world. Inventory is used in these cases to maintain continuity of supply. Stockpiling might be advantageous depending on the volatility of the supply conditions.

Customer Requirements

There are several questions regarding customer requirements whose answer will affect inventory decisions. Is the item make-to-order or make-to-stock? How much customization is allowed? End items that are standard with no customization can be inventoried to meet uncertain demand. If the end item is assembled to order, inventory is best maintained in the form of subassemblies that can be combined to customer order. In both cases, raw material and component inventories can be maintained based on planned usage. If the end item is custom manufactured from standard materials, inventory control is focused on the availability of raw materials and components. If each order is custom, including materials and components, inventory is primarily a function of the production planning and manufacturing processes.

Source

The first consideration relating to source is whether the item is internally supplied or purchased from a source outside the firm or both. An internally supplied item may contend with other items for production capacity, thereby requiring higher inventory levels than with an external supplier. For items that can be produced internally or purchased, many issues affect the decision, with inventory requirements being only one.

The second consideration is whether the supplier is domestic or international. The use of international suppliers has the potential to increase the uncertainty in the supply process, especially lead times, creating the need for higher safety stock levels.

A third consideration is the geographical location of the supplier. It may be advantageous to group items by supplier and geographical area to allow the buyer to take advantage of joint product quantity discounts or transportation pooling.

Material State

Material state information includes shelf life and stock rotation requirements. Items with a short shelf life require close management to ensure that inventory levels are closely monitored to prevent spoilage and obsolescence. Also, the inventory control system must ensure that stock is rotated so that the oldest stock is used first.

Performance Measures

Inventory management practices are profoundly affected by how an inventory manager is evaluated. If service level is the key measure of performance, the strategy would favor carrying more inventory. If inventory level or turns is the performance measure, there would be a tendency to sacrifice service to keep the investment lower. Appropriate performance measures can be devised only after answering the question of how inventory helps the firm to compete or add value to the customer. Performance measures for inventory managers must be consistent with the objectives and competitive advantages of having inventories.

MEASURING INVENTORY PERFORMANCE

A tool that is useful in determining the appropriate control systems and performance measures is the ABC classification. Once inventories have been classified, there are two types of performance measures for evaluating inventory performance. The first class is based on the quantity of inventory and the second is based on the service level provided to the customer.

ABC Classification

The ABC classification is based on the Pareto Rule (also called the 80/20 Rule), which says that 80 percent of the value of an inventory can be found in 20 percent of the part numbers. The ABC classification expands the concept into three groups. A items are the high-value and/or high-volume items that normally account for 40 to 50 percent of the inventory value and 10 to 20 percent of the part numbers. B items are those with moderate value and/or volume. They generally run 20 to 40 percent of inventory value and 20 to 40 percent of the part numbers. C items, the low-value and/or low-volume items, are 10 to 20 percent of inventory value and 40 to 60 percent of the part numbers. Table 2.1 presents example data. The top part of Table 2.1 gives the sales data for the various items and the percentage of the total sales of each item. The bottom part of the table shows the results after the items have been prioritized based on total sales. The top four items in terms of sales are classified as A items and comprise 20 percent of the part numbers and 55.4 percent of the total sales. The next six items, classified as B items, account for 30 percent of the part numbers and 28.9 percent of the total sales. The remaining ten items are classified as C items and account for only 15.7 percent of the total sales.

The value of ABC classification is to prioritize managerial effort for applying resources for monitoring and reducing inventory. A 10-percent reduction in the total C item value nets only a 1- to 2-percent savings while the same reduction on A items nets a 4- to 5-percent savings. Therefore, it gives

TABLE 2.1

ABC Classification Example

Part No.	Description	Sales	Sales Units	Percent Total $ Usage	Percent Total Unit Usage
1	Anodes, acid—fine copper	$ 279,273	955	4.2	1.8
2	Calcium chloride	87,104	1,028	1.3	1.9
3	Caustic soda	861,221	3,922	12.9	7.4
4	Citric acid—fine	82,675	8,705	1.2	16.5
5	Clearon CDB	247,140	358	3.7	0.7
6	Cream of tartar	125,607	2,188	1.9	4.1
7	Hydrogen peroxide 35% tech.	36,394	2,055	0.5	3.9
8	Igepal CO 630	191,200	1,348	2.9	2.5
9	Isopropyl alcohol	983,175	2,811	14.7	5.3
10	Monoethanolamine	925,102	1,036	13.8	2.0
11	Nitric acid 42BE	361,120	1,419	5.4	2.7
12	Pumice 4F	60,545	1,775	0.9	3.4
13	Silicone AF93	65,381	1,258	1.0	2.4
14	Sodium bicarb USP pwd #1	935,129	5,838	14.0	11.0
15	Sodium carbonate monohydrate	74,375	2,388	1.1	4.5
16	Sodium metasulfite anyh. FG	297,108	4,788	4.4	9.1
17	Sulfuric acid 66BE	337,166	4,169	5.0	7.9
18	Sulfuric acid 98%	73,154	2,407	1.1	4.6
19	Tartaric acid FCC	417,536	3,854	6.2	7.3
20	UCAR food freeze 35	242,941	577	3.6	1.1
	Total	$ 6,683,346	52,879		

Resulting ABC Classification

Class	Part Number	Percentage of Total Items	Percentage of Total Dollar Usage
A	3, 9, 10, 14	20	55.4
B	1, 5, 11, 16, 18, 19	30	28.9
C	2, 4, 6, 7, 8, 12, 13, 15, 17, 20	50	15.7

the manager guidance as to where to begin looking for improvements. The ABC classification may also give rise to the use of different performance measures. Service level measures might be more appropriate for A items while an inventory level measure such as turns might be better for C items.

Inventory Investment

The inventory investment is a common concern of many managers. A telephone survey of *Cash Flow Enhancement Report* readers indicated that 23 percent of the respondents cited stock turnover as their second highest priority for enhancing cash flow.[5] This is consistent with research by Buddress and Raedels on purchasing performance measures where inventory performance was ranked second in importance in departmental and seventh in personal performance measures.[6] Common measures of inventory performance included the number of inventory turns, level of inventory, and number of days in stock. Inventory turns are calculated by dividing the cost of goods for a time period, usually annually, by the average inventory value for the time period. This can be calculated on an aggregate basis, by product line, or by individual item. For example, the inventory turnover ratio for the fabricated metals industry is 8.6 turns per year while the printing industry's ratio is 18.9 turns per year. The number of days in stock is measured by dividing the inventory level by the average usage per day. This is usually best done on an item-by-item basis and works best if based on the number of units rather than on dollars. There is a real danger in using aggregate numbers for turnover or number of days in stock, as items that are poor performers are not identified. For example, assume a firm has an average of 20 days' stock on hand. That could be 100 items each with 20 days' stock on hand or it could be 70 items with 5 days' stock on hand and 30 items with 90 days' stock on hand. Clearly the second scenario indicates a large number of items with an inventory problem. There is no magic number for acceptable levels of inventory other than smaller is better from a financial point of view. Each manager must consider all the dimensions including cost, service level, availability of goods, market

---

[5] "IRR Miscellany," *Inventory Reduction Report,* 93 (2) (February 1993), p 9.

[6] Leland Buddress and Alan Raedels, "Measuring Purchasing Performance: A TQM Approach," *Logistics: Navigating the Future,* 78th Annual International Purchasing Conference Proceedings (Tempe, Ariz.: National Association of Purchasing Management, 1993), pp. 162–167.

conditions, seasonality, and capacity. Table 2.2 presents recent inventory turnover data for a variety of industries. The low column represents the low median turnover ratio observed, and the high column is the highest median turnover ratio observed for a four-digit Standard Industrial Classification (SIC) code within that industry. The median column is the median of the median turnover ratios for the four-digit SIC codes within the industry.

TABLE 2.2
Standard Industry Inventory Ratios

Industry	Median Cost of Sales/ Inventory Value		
	Low	*Median*	*High*
Nonmanufacturing			
Mining	4.6	16.5	45.0
Construction	3.0	39.2	95.2
Transportation	6.9	56.0	371.8
Communications	14.1	29.6	94.0
Utilities	13.8	37.1	83.9
Wholesale trade			
Durable	2.7	8.2	22.0
Nondurable	7.3	12.5	74.4
Retail trade	2.5	6.1	108.4
Manufacturing			
Food processing	1.5	14.3	43.4
Textile mills	4.6	9.8	17.6
Apparel	2.4	7.6	21.5
Lumber & wood products	6.9	12.9	25.1
Furniture	8.4	10.7	21.4
Paper & allied products	8.1	12.4	20.5
Printing	5.1	18.9	71.3
Chemicals	4.5	8.8	13.9
Petroleum & related	9.6	12.9	28.3
Rubber & plastics	7.2	11.7	18.7
Leather	3.6	7.2	11.1
Stone, clay, & glass	5.5	11.3	55.6
Primary metals	5.9	12.1	53.4
Fabricated metals	5.1	8.6	46.5
Machinery	5.1	8.2	25.7
Electrical machinery	4.0	7.6	14.7
Transportation machinery	4.7	7.3	44.8
Instruments	5.0	7.0	10.5

Source: *Industry Norms and Key Business Ratios* (Murray Hill, N.J.: Dun & Bradstreet, Inc., 1993).

Service Level

One reason for having inventory is to avoid a stockout that results in an unplanned changeover, shutdown, or lost sale. One obvious measure of service level is the number of unplanned changeovers and shutdowns caused by lack of inventory. The difficulty comes in trying to specify an appropriate measure. One class of measures is percentage based. For example, suppose 50 customers each order two line items from a firm. One item has a quantity of 90 units and the second, 10 units. If only one of the 50 orders cannot be filled because only nine units of the second item are available, the service level is 98 percent based on the number of orders filled. If the unit of measure is changed from number of orders to number of line items, the service level goes from 49 out of 50 to 99 out of 100 or 99 percent. If the unit of measure is expanded to the number of units shipped, the service level goes to 4,999 out of 5,000 or 99.98 percent. Thus the problem with percentage-based measures is that the choice of the unit of measure will affect the performance level.

TABLE 2.3

Example Percentage- and Absolute-Based Measures of Inventory Service Level

---

Percentage-Based Measures

Percentage of overdue orders
Percentage of stockouts caused by late deliveries
Percentage of stockouts caused by underbuying
Percentage of order periods without a stockout
Percentage of order periods with a stockout
Percentage of units supplied on time
Percentage of line items supplied on time
Percentage of operating days without a stockout
Percentage of inventory value declared obsolete

Absolute-Based Measures

Number of production stoppages caused by late deliveries
Actual expediting expense
Number of order periods without a stockout
Number of order periods with a stockout
Number of operating days without a stockout
Dollar value of obsolete items

An alternate approach is to use absolute-based measures. Using the same example, you could say there was one incomplete order, one line item not available, or one unit not available. Table 2.3 presents a variety of both absolute- and percentage-based measures of service level.

MAINTAINING INVENTORY RECORD ACCURACY

In any inventory system, accurate information is essential for good decision making. Two key tools used for keeping inventory information current are cycle counting and the use of bar coding technology.

Periodic Versus Cycle Counting

Periodic control means taking a physical inventory on a regular basis. That timing could be as frequently as monthly but more often is semiannually or annually. This involves having individuals go through and identify everything within the inventory and its quantity. The problem is that the inventory records are never accurate, since by the time a discrepancy is noted and corrected, one or more transactions may have taken place, changing the data and introducing the possibility of more error. Additionally, full physical inventories are time consuming and are often inaccurate.

An alternate approach is cycle counting. Cycle counting is based on the fact that the probability of an error in inventory data is directly related to the number of transactions that take place within a time period. The greater the number of transactions, the greater the probability of an error taking place. Therefore, items that are used more frequently or are of high value should be counted more frequently than items that are used infrequently or are of low value. Using the ABC classification of inventory, a cycle counting system might have the A items counted monthly, the B items counted quarterly, and the C items counted semiannually or annually. Other trigger mechanisms for cycle counting include the receipt of an item, a negative or zero balance reported in the inventory report, the passage of a specified number of inventory transactions, or the passage of time, such as every other day counting shelf stock in a grocery store.

Bar Coding

A tool for inventory control that is gaining more popularity, especially as the hardware costs continue to decline, is the use of bar codes. Bar codes are alternating patterns of light and dark lines that are used to represent letters and numbers. As light is reflected by the white spaces and absorbed by the dark lines; the reflected light is read by a sensor, which translates the pattern into the appropriate letter or number. There are several one-dimensional codes: Universal Product Code, 2-of-5, Codabar, and Code 39, also called Logmars by the federal government. There are also two-dimensional coding systems for use when the amount of information required exceeds one bar's capacity. The stacked bar system uses several bars placed one above the other to represent the required information. The system software must be programmed to read and interpret the bars in the proper order. Each bar uses one of the standard one-dimensional bar codes. The matrix system uses dots at particular locations in a matrix to represent the relevant information.

The scanners used to read the bar codes can be of two basic types, fixed position and hand held. Fixed position scanners are mounted in one location and the label must pass by the scanner to be read. For example, the railroads have mounted fixed scanners designed to read the bar codes on each railroad car to log in its location, date, and time as the train passes by the scanner. Another example is the scanner used in supermarket checkout stands.

Hand held scanners can be of two types, those that require direct contact with the label and those that don't. Direct contact scanners are generally lighter in weight than noncontact scanners since the light source does not have to be as large.

Bar codes bring a variety of benefits to inventory control. First, they facilitate data entry. A bar code scan is 75 percent faster than typing and 33 percent faster than entering the data on a 10-key pad. Second, they improve data quality, with accuracy rates around one error per million characters.[7] Third, the availability of current data improves scheduling and ordering decisions since they are made with timely and more accurate information.

PURCHASING'S ROLE IN INVENTORY MANAGEMENT

Purchasing's role in inventory management will vary depending on the nature of the business. In manufacturing, purchasing's major inventory

---

[7]Susan Avery, "Bar codes take off from factory floor," *Purchasing,* November 7, 1991, p. 52.

concerns are with raw materials and components, MRO, and office supplies. In the wholesale and retail industries, buyers have much more responsibility for inventory and service levels. In health care, the majority of items are supplies and may or may not be under purchasing's control. The recent job analysis of purchasing, which was done in preparation for revising the Certified Purchasing Manager Examination, indicates that the control of inventory storage, data discrepancies, and stock rotation was a responsibility of 50 to 60 percent of the respondents. The largest responses were in retail and state and local government. However, at the same time the level of importance was generally low, with average responses between two and three on a scale of one to seven with one indicating low importance.[8] This is also reflected in the 1988 CAPS (Center for Advanced Purchasing Studies) study of purchasing organizational relationships, where 37 percent of the respondents indicated that inventory control reported to purchasing. Only 35 percent of the manufacturing respondents indicated that inventory control reported to purchasing as opposed to 55 percent of service sector respondents.[9]

In general purchasing can undertake several activities to help reduce inventories. The first area is in the prompt disposition of reject and obsolete materials. These items can be returned to the supplier, transferred to other users within the firm, or disposed of as scrap. A second area is in keeping lead time estimates as accurate as possible. If lead time estimates are high, the firm is receiving material before it is needed, causing higher inventory levels. If lead time estimates are low, inventories may not be adequate, causing increased stockout-related costs. A third area that has received more attention recently is the use of consignment inventories. The advantage of consignment inventories is that the firm doesn't incur the cost of the consigned goods until they are used, thus reducing the firm's inventory investment. However, other inventory costs may still exist. Consignment inventories are really a means of sharing inventory carrying costs between the buyer and seller. A fourth area, which is becoming common purchasing practice, is to make use of systems contracts. Systems contracts allow the requisitioner to order

---

[8]Eugene W. Muller, *Job Analysis Identifying the Tasks of Purchasing* (Tempe, Ariz.: Center for Advanced Purchasing Studies, 1992), p. 40.

[9]Harold E. Fearon, *Purchasing Organizational Relationships* (Tempe, Ariz.: Center for Advanced Purchasing Studies, 1988), pp. 14–15.

what is needed, when it is needed. The 24-hour turnaround time typically available under systems contracts minimizes the need for inventories of those items. Major areas of application include office supplies and MRO items.

CHAPTER SUMMARY

This chapter has examined the roles and costs of inventory within the firm. Key points are:

- Inventory exists in many forms, including raw materials, components, work-in-process, finished goods, MRO, and resale goods.
- The functions of inventory include protection from uncertainty of supply and demand, anticipation of special events, consideration of economies of scale, decoupling operations, and transportation of material from one location to another.
- The costs of inventory include carrying, ordering, stockout, and product costs.
- The decisions regarding what items and how much to stock of an item are dependent upon item value, demand patterns, availability, customer requirements, source, material state, and how inventory performance is measured.
- Inventories can be classified based on value and volume of consumption using the ABC classification system to guide the manager in determining the appropriate control systems and performance measures.
- Inventory performance measures can be based upon the inventory investment or service level.
- Inventory record accuracy is best maintained using cycle counting techniques. The use of bar codes is highly beneficial in improving data collection accuracy.
- Purchasing's role in inventory management includes reducing order processing time and costs, maintaining accurate lead time information, working with suppliers to find alternate approaches for supply such as consignment inventories, and promoting the use of systems contracts to reduce on-site inventory requirements.

- Last, and most important, although inventory levels can be reduced through tighter controls, the real gains come by better management of the supply processes. The major reductions in inventory costs are not made by managing inventories but by improving supply processes.

REFERENCES

Baker, R. Jerry, Lee Buddress, and Robert S. Kuehne. *Policy and Procedures Manual for Purchasing and Materials Control,* 2nd ed. Englewood Cliffs, N.J.: Prentice Hall, 1992.

Industry Norms and Key Business Ratios. Murray Hill, N.J.: Dun & Bradstreet, Inc., 1993.

Inventory Reduction Report. New York: Institute of Management and Administration, Inc., 1993.

Lambert, Douglas M., and James R. Stock. *Strategic Logistics Management,* 3rd ed. Homewood, Ill.: Irwin, 1993.

Plossl, George W. *Production and Inventory Control: Principles and Techniques,* 2nd ed. Englewood Cliffs, N.J.: Prentice Hall, Inc., 1985.

Vollmann, Thomas E., William L. Berry, and D. Clay Whybark. *Manufacturing Planning and Control Systems,* 3rd ed. Homewood, Ill.: Irwin, 1992.

CHAPTER 3

MANAGING INDEPENDENT DEMAND INVENTORY SYSTEMS

INTRODUCTION

Pfizer Pharmaceuticals, a large, vertically integrated chemical manufacturer, saw a need to develop an inventory management system to improve inventory turnover and accuracy and reduce swings in inventory levels across multiple divisions. The application of detailed inventory models and techniques led to a reduction in inventories of $23.1 million over a three-year period. This resulted in annual savings of $3.6 million in carrying costs, annual setup cost reductions of $250,000, reduced freight costs of $280,000 annually, and an increase in customer service to 99.98 percent.[1]

The proper application of an independent demand inventory system can mean significant savings, as illustrated by the example above. Independent demand inventory systems are based on the premise that the demand or usage of a particular item is independent of the demand or usage of other items. Inventory types that can be managed with independent demand systems include most finished goods, spare parts, MRO, and resale inventories. Items whose demand or usage is related to other products such as raw materials, component parts, and work-in-process inventories are often better managed using the dependent demand systems, which are presented in Chapter 4.

Independent demand inventory systems are pull systems. Pull systems pull material from the previous operation as it is needed to replace

---

[1]James R. Evans, *Applied Production and Operations Management,* 4th ed. (St. Paul, Minn.: West Publishing Company, 1993), pp. 491–493.

materials that have been used. In the case of finished goods, a pull system authorizes the production of finished goods to replace products as they are sold. The independent demand inventory models answer the question of when to place the replenishment order and how much to order at one time.

There are two factors for classifying independent demand inventory systems as shown in Table 3.1. They are the review mechanism and the order quantity. The review mechanism deals with when to check the inventory to see if more stock is required. There are two basic approaches, continuous and periodic review. The second factor that determines the basic nature of the inventory system is whether the order quantity is fixed or varies from order to order. Within each of the four classes of models that these two factors create, the manager must also be concerned with how to determine the reorder point and the safety stock.

The first two factors form the structure of this chapter. The chapter begins with a discussion of continuous review models and periodic review models with fixed and variable order quantities. This is followed by a discussion of independent demand inventory models in a distribution and a just-in-time setting. Last, the problems in managing and maintaining independent demand inventory systems will be discussed along with their implications for purchasing.

CONTINUOUS REVIEW SYSTEMS

Continuous review systems are inventory control systems that monitor the level of inventory every time an inventory transaction takes place. When

TABLE 3.1

Independent Demand Inventory Systems

	Review Frequency	
Order Quantity	Continuous review Fixed order quantity	Periodic review Fixed order quantity
	Continuous review Variable order quantity	Periodic review Variable order quantity

the inventory of an item reaches a critical level, called the reorder point, a replenishment order is placed. These models are often called reorder point models, reflecting the order process.

Continuous review models are useful for items at all levels of ABC classifications. They are relatively easy to use and can be easily automated. Since they monitor every inventory transaction, the chances of a stockout (assuming that nothing in the supply process changes) are relatively low. This allows the monitoring and controlling of a large number of items relatively easily.

The weaknesses of continuous review or reorder point models are best illustrated with a simple example. You are about to drive to the top of Pike's Peak in Colorado. However, before you begin your journey a few minor modifications will be made to your car. First, the front windshield will be painted black and your sunroof and side windows will be sealed shut so you cannot see where you are going. Next, your transmission will be locked in drive so you cannot back up the hill, and last your throttle will be fixed at 45 miles per hour. Now have a safe trip! As you try to ascend the mountain you find you can make corrections only when you pass a point. When you see the sign that says "Curve," you are probably too late to make a correction. This is the difficulty with order point systems. The actions taken today are based on what happened yesterday, or at best today, and do not consider the future. These models assume that the past will predict the future. Additionally, since order point systems react only to past events, they are not able to give information on future orders to be released after the current order. Therefore, continuous review models are most appropriate when the past is a good indicator of the future demand or usage of an item. This is the case with mature products with stable demand or items with regular usage such as production supplies or forms.

In this section we will look at two classes of continuous review models, fixed order quantity and variable order quantity. Under the fixed order quantity we will develop four standard forms.

Fixed Order Quantity Models

This section develops four standard forms of fixed order quantity models. These are economic order quantity, noninstantaneous replenishment economic order quantity, economic order quantity with price discounts, and economic order quantity with uncertain demand. The first three models assume conditions of certainty to simplify the mathematics. Although conditions of certainty are seldom valid assumptions, we start here for two reasons. One, it is easier to begin with a simple model and then relax the various assumptions; and two, when the quantity ordered is relatively large compared with the daily demand, these models have been shown to have a fairly wide range of application in spite of their assumptions.

Economic Order Quantity Model

The economic order quantity (EOQ) model determines the amount of an item to order, which minimizes the total inventory costs for that item. By minimizing the total costs, the model is able to find the order quantity that considers the tradeoffs between the carrying and ordering costs. Table 3.2 lists the assumptions and variables used in developing the model. Independent demand means that the demand for an item is independent of the demand for any other item and is not related to the demand in a previous period. Constant lead time means that the time from placing an order

TABLE 3.2
Economic Order Quantity Model

Assumptions

Independent demand
Constant lead time
Constant costs (product, holding, and ordering)
Constant demand
Instantaneous replenishment

Variables

i = Carrying cost as a percent of product value (%/unit/period)
c = Product cost or value ($/unit)
H = Carrying cost in $/unit/period = $(i)(c)$
S = Order or setup cost ($/order)
D = Demand per period (units/period)
L = Lead time (periods)
R = Reorder point (units)
Q = Quantity ordered

Model

$$Q = \sqrt{\frac{2DS}{H}}$$

$$R = DL$$

to receiving an order does not change. Constant costs means that the cost do not change with changes in the size or frequency of the orders. Instantaneous replenishment means that after an order is placed, the entire order is received at one point in time, causing the inventory level to increase instantaneously by the order quantity. The time frame for the demand and the carrying costs is traditionally given as annual. Technically all the model requires is that the time frames for demand and carrying costs be the same. Daily, weekly, monthly, quarterly, or annually, it does not matter as long as the two use the same time frame.

Figure 3.1 shows what the process will look like over time. As an order is received, Q units will go into inventory. The inventory will deplete by D units per period on a constant rate. When the reorder point is reached, an order is placed for Q units, which is received after L periods. The order arrives at the receiving dock just as the last unit in inventory is used.

The first step in deriving the optimal order quantity that minimizes the firm's total cost is to develop the total cost equation. The total cost for a period is the total product cost plus the total order cost plus the total

FIGURE 3.1
Economic Order Quantity Model

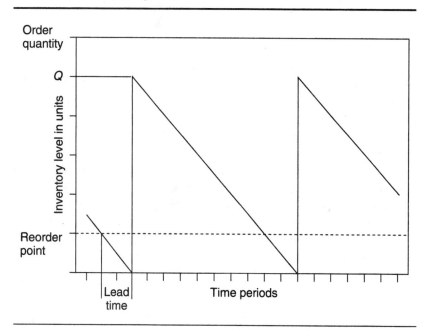

holding cost plus the total stockout cost. If the lead time is constant and demand is constant, an order for Q units will be placed when the inventory level reaches the reorder point R, and thus, a stockout will not occur. The stockout costs then become zero and can be ignored. Using the variables listed in Table 3.2, the total cost equation is:

$$\text{Total cost} = cD + \frac{D}{Q}S + \frac{Q}{2}H \qquad (3.1)$$

The first term, $[cD]$, is the total product cost, cost per unit times the demand in units per period. The second term, $[(D/Q)S]$, is the total ordering cost and/or setup cost as discussed in Chapter 2. The term (D/Q) is the demand in units per period divided by the quantity per order in units per order, giving the total number of orders per period, which is then multiplied by the cost per order. The third term, $[(Q/2)H]$, is the total carrying costs. The $(Q/2)$ term is the average inventory on hand at any time, which is multiplied by the carrying cost per unit per period, H. To find the optimal value of Q that minimizes the total cost, take the first derivative of the total cost equation with respect to Q, set it equal to zero, and solve for Q. The resulting formula is

$$Q = \sqrt{\frac{2DS}{H}} \qquad (3.2)$$

As the demand increases, the order quantity will increase by the square root. For example, if demand doubled, the order quantity would increase by 41 percent. The only ways to reduce the order quantity, given a specific demand level, are to lower the order or setup costs or increase the carrying costs.

For example, in a chemical distribution firm, the demand for five-gallon containers of acetone is 40 containers per day. The purchasing department estimates the cost of placing a purchase order at $75 per order and the carrying cost at $0.01 per container per day. Applying the EOQ model, the demand per period, D, would be 40 containers per day; the order cost, S, would be $75 per order; and the carrying cost, H, would be $0.01 per container per day. The order quantity is

$$Q = \sqrt{\frac{(2)(40)(75)}{(0.01)}} = 775 \text{ containers} \qquad (3.3)$$

A relatively simple fixed order quantity model is the two bin system. In the two bin system, an item is stored in two bins or containers. When the first container or bin is emptied, an order is placed for enough material to fill two bins. The second bin is used while awaiting the delivery of the order. When the order is received, it is hoped before the second bin is emptied, both containers are filled and the first container is again used to meet demand. The problem with this system is ensuring that the order is placed when the first bin is emptied. Without individual responsibility or if users do not understand their responsibilities, it is very easy to wind up with two empty containers and no order placed.

Noninstantaneous Replenishment Economic Order Quantity Model

The noninstantaneous replenishment economic order quantity model assumes that material is received into inventory over a period of time, gradually building up the inventory rather than instantly as in the EOQ model. Table 3.3 lists the assumptions and variables that will be used in developing the model. The only other change in assumptions from the EOQ model is that the production rate or the rate at which material is received from a supplier is greater than the demand rate. If this were not true, then the inventory would not build up.

Figure 3.2 shows what the process will look like over time. As an order is received, inventory is built up at the rate of *(P – D)* units for *t* periods. The inventory will then deplete at a constant rate of *D* units per period. When the reorder point is reached, an order is placed for *Q* units, which is received after *L* periods. The order is received into inventory just as the last unit in inventory is used.

The derivation of the optimal order quantity that minimizes the firm's total cost is the same as for the EOQ model. Using the variables listed in Table 3.3, the total cost equation is

$$\text{Total cost} = cD + \frac{D}{Q}S + \frac{(P-D)t}{2}H \qquad (3.4)$$

The first two terms are the same as in the EOQ model. This equation cannot be solved for Q yet because there are two unknowns, t and Q. The total amount produced will be Q which is the production rate *(P)* times the

TABLE 3.3

Noninstantaneous Replenishment EOQ Model

Assumptions

Independent demand
Constant lead time
Constant costs (product, ordering, and carrying)
Constant demand
Noninstantaneous replenishment
Production rate exceeds demand rate

Variables

P = Production rate per period (units/period)
i = Carrying cost as a percent of product value (%/unit/period)
c = Product cost or value ($/unit)
H = Carrying cost in $/unit/period = $(i)(c)$
S = Order or setup cost ($/order)
D = Demand per period (units/period)
L = Lead time (periods)
R = Reorder point (units)
Q = Quantity ordered
t = Number of periods product is produced

Model

$$Q = \sqrt{\frac{2DS}{H} \quad \frac{P}{(P-D)}}$$

$$R = DL$$

number of periods the item is produced *(t)*, giving $Q = Pt$. Solving for
t gives $t = Q/P$, and substituting for t in the total cost equation gives

$$\text{Total cost} = cD + \frac{D}{Q}S + \frac{(P-D)}{P}\frac{Q}{2}H \qquad (3.5)$$

Taking the first derivative of the total cost equation with respect to Q, setting it equal to zero, and solving for Q gives the value of Q, which minimizes the total costs. The resulting formula is

$$Q = \sqrt{\frac{2DS}{H} \quad \frac{P}{(P-D)}} \qquad (3.6)$$

FIGURE 3.2
Noninstantaneous Replenishment Model

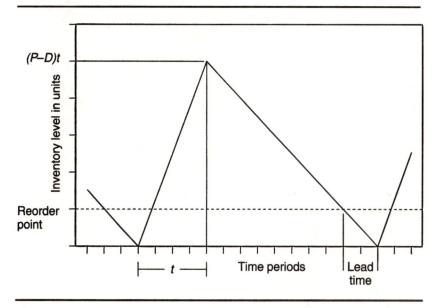

For example, a manufacturing firm has a spare part with a demand of 40 units per day. When the spare part is manufactured, it can be produced at a rate of 100 units per day. The order cost is $75 per order and the estimated carrying cost is $0.01 per unit per day. Applying the noninstantaneous model, the demand per period, D, is 40 units per day; the production rate, P, is 100 units per day; the order cost, S, is $75 per order; and the carrying cost, H, is $0.01 per unit per day. The optimal order quantity is

$$Q = \sqrt{\frac{(2)(40)(75)}{(0.01)} \quad \frac{(100)}{(100-40)}} = 1000 \text{ units} \qquad (3.7)$$

The maximum inventory level will reach only 600 units since part of each day's production is used to meet that day's demand.

Price Discount Model
The price discount model relaxes the assumption of constant product cost. In this model, it is assumed that the product cost will vary with the quantity ordered. The starting point for this model is the EOQ model. However,

the EOQ model ignores the product cost in finding the optimal order quantity. Thus the price discount model adds a second step to compare the total costs of the EOQ model with the total cost of ordering the minimum amount required to obtain the next lowest price. Table 3.4 shows the assumptions and variables.

Starting with the basic EOQ model, (ic_j) is substituted for H since the carrying cost as a percent of product value, i, is constant but the product cost may vary with the order quantity. This gives the optimal order quantity formula

$$Q_j = \sqrt{\frac{2DS}{ic_j}} \qquad (3.8)$$

TABLE 3.4
Price Discount Model

Assumptions

Independent demand
Constant lead time
Constant order costs
Constant demand
Instantaneous replenishment
Product cost varies with order quantity

Variables

i = Carrying cost as a percent of product value (%/unit/period)
c_j = Product cost for quantity range j
H = Carrying cost in \$/unit/period = $(i)(c)$
S = Order or setup cost (\$/order)
D = Demand per period (units/period)
L = Lead time (periods)
R = Reorder point (units)
Q = Quantity ordered

Model

$$Q_j = \sqrt{\frac{2DS}{ic_j}}$$

$$R = DL$$

The first step in determining the optimal order quantity is to calculate the value of Q_j for each price range to find the value of Q_j which is consistent with the price c_j—that is, where the quantity to be ordered can be ordered at the cost used in calculating the optimal order quantity. The most efficient process is to start with the lowest price and work up until a feasible combination is found. The second step is to calculate the total cost using the optimal value of Q_i and a minimum value for Q, which will obtain the next lower price. The quantity that gives the lowest total cost is the amount to order. The rationale of the price discount model is that the savings in the product cost may more than offset the increased carrying costs of a larger order quantity.

For example, a hospital uses 2,000 reams of paper per year. The price per ream from the distributor varies depending on the quantity ordered at one time.

Reams	Price ($) per Ream
1–999	2.00
100–499	1.90
500–999	1.80
1,000 or more	1.70

The order cost is $75 per purchase order issued and the carrying charge is estimated at 25 percent of the ream's cost per year. Applying the price discount model, the demand per period, D, is 2,000 reams per year; the order cost, S, is $75 per order; and the carrying charge, i, is 25 percent per ream per year. The first step is to calculate the optimal order quantity for the lowest price range of $1.70 per ream.

$$Q_1 = \sqrt{\frac{(2)(2000)(75)}{(.25)(1.70)}} = 840 \text{ reams} \qquad (3.9)$$

This quantity is not feasible, as ordering 840 reams does not qualify for a price of $1.70 per ream. Next, calculate the economic order quantity using the next higher price of $1.80 per ream.

$$Q_2 = \sqrt{\frac{(2)(2000)(75)}{(.25)(1.80)}} = 816 \text{ reams} \qquad (3.10)$$

This quantity is feasible; therefore, proceed to the second step and calculate the total costs of ordering 816 reams at a time, and 1,000 reams at a time which is the minimum quantity that can be ordered to obtain the next lowest price.

$$TC_{816} = (2000)(\$1.80) + \frac{(2000)}{(816)}(\$75) + \frac{(816)}{(2)}(.25)(\$1.80) = \$3,967.42$$

$$(3.11)$$

$$TC_{1000} = (2000)(\$1.70) + \frac{(2000)}{(1000)}(\$75) + \frac{(1000)}{(2)}(.25)(\$1.70) = \$3,762.50$$

$$(3.12)$$

Therefore, ordering 1,000 reams at a time is a lower cost solution than ordering 816 reams at a time because the savings from the price discount exceed the increases in carrying costs for the larger order quantity.

Economic Order Quantity Model with Uncertain Demand

This model begins with the EOQ model but relaxes the assumption of constant demand. The model assumes that the period demand is now normally distributed with mean $\overline{D}$ and variance σ^2 and that the distribution is the same each period. Since the mean is the best estimate of demand in any period, the optimal order quantity is the same as in the EOQ model. The difference comes in the reorder point calculation. As lead time is still constant, reordering when the inventory reaches $\overline{D}L$ gives a 50 percent chance that the demand will be greater than the inventory on hand. Therefore, to reduce the probability of stocking out, a safety or buffer stock is employed. The amount of safety stock depends on what probability of a stockout which is acceptable to management. Since the demand per period is normally distributed, the distribution of the demand during the lead time will also be normally distributed with mean, $(\overline{D}L)$ and variance, $\sigma^2 L$. Since the firm is concerned only when demand is greater than $\overline{D}L$, it is necessary to use only the number of standard deviations on the plus side of the mean. For example, for a 95-percent coverage, i.e. a 5-percent stockout probability, only 1.645 standard deviations above the mean are required. The resulting formula for the reorder point then is

$$R = \overline{D}L + z\sigma\sqrt{L} \qquad (3.13)$$

For example, an electric utility's maintenance department has an average demand for an item of 174 units per week with a standard deviation of 18 units per week. The cost to place an order is $75 per order, the estimated carrying cost is $0.03 per unit per week, and it takes two weeks to receive replacement parts. The maintenance department desires to provide a 95 percent service level on parts availability. Applying the uncertain demand model, the average demand per period, $\bar{D}$, is 174 units per week with a standard deviation, σ, of 18 units per week; the order cost, S, is $75 per order; the carrying cost, H, is $0.03 per unit per week; and the lead time, L, is two weeks. Additionally, the desired probability of a stockout is 5 percent. The optimal order quantity then is

$$Q = \sqrt{\frac{(2)(174)(75)}{(0.03)}} = 932 \text{ units} \qquad (3.14)$$

and the reorder point is

$$R = (174)(2) + (1.645)(18)\sqrt{(2)} = 348 + 42 = 390 \text{ units} \qquad (3.15)$$

The safety stock is 42 units, giving a 95-percent service level. If the service level were increased to 99 percent, the multiplier would increase from 1.645 to 2.33, giving a new safety stock of 59 units and a reorder point of 407 units.

Variable Order Quantity

The variable order quantity model orders a variable quantity when the inventory level crosses the reorder point. The quantity to be ordered can be established in several ways. One approach is to set the quantity to be ordered based on the amount of shelf space available. The quantity ordered could be based either on the difference between the space available and the quantity on hand at the time of order or on the expected difference between the space available and the anticipated space available when the order is received. The advantage to the variable order quantity model is that special circumstances such as seasonality or large sales can be taken into account when placing orders. A second approach is to specify a maximum inventory level allowed for an item based on demand or a desired inventory turnover rate.

FIGURE 3.1
EOQ Model with Uncertain Demand

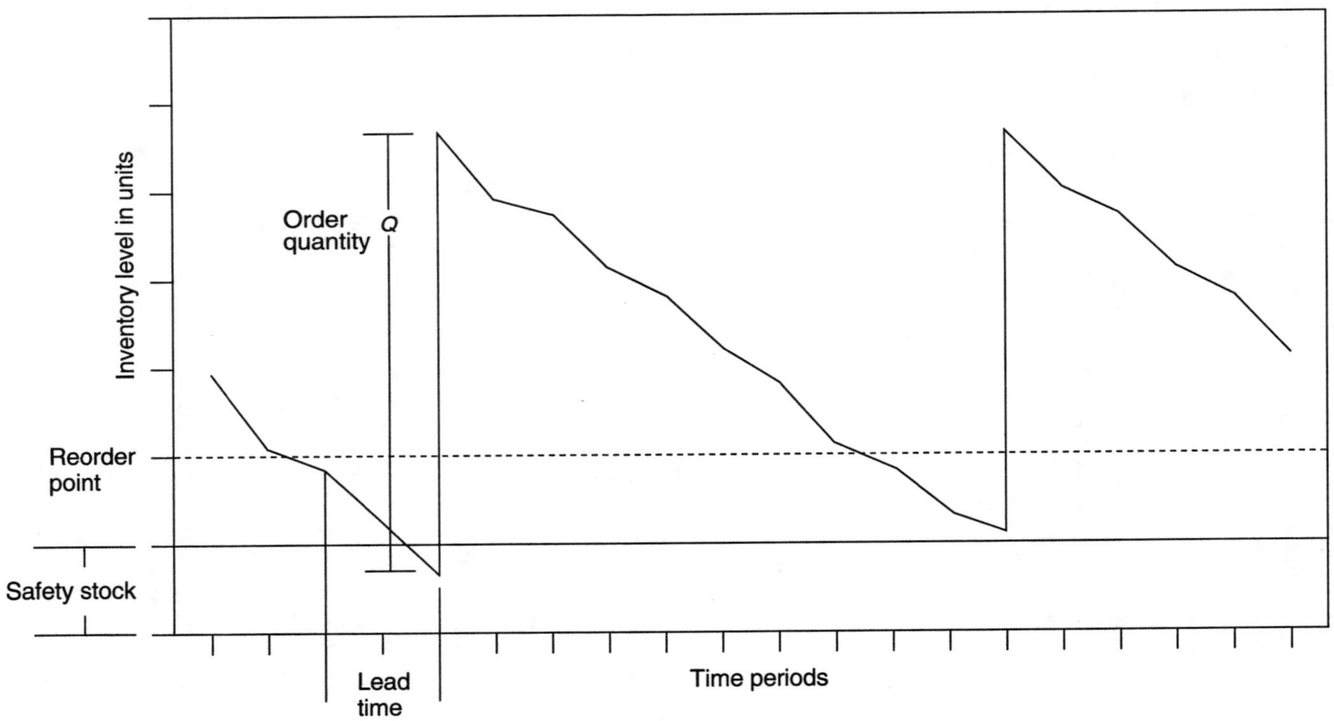

TABLE 3.5
Economic Order Quantity with Uncertain Demand Model

Assumptions

Independent demand
Constant lead time
Constant costs (product, ordering, carrying)
Demand follows normal distribution
Instantaneous replenishment

Variables

i = Carrying cost as a percent of product value (%/unit/period)
c = Product cost or value ($/unit)
H = Carrying cost in $/unit/period = $(i)(c)$
S = Order or setup cost ($/order)
$\bar{D}$ = Average demand per period (units/period)
σ = Standard deviation of demand (units/period)
L = Lead time (periods)
R = Reorder point (units)
Q = Quantity ordered
z = Number of standard deviations required to give desired service level

Model

$$Q = \sqrt{\frac{2\bar{D}S}{H}}$$

$$R = \bar{D}L + z\sigma\sqrt{L}$$

PERIODIC REVIEW SYSTEMS

Periodic review systems check the inventory level on a periodic basis as opposed to a transaction basis. Thus inventory levels need to be verified only periodically rather than continually, reducing the control costs. Periodic review systems are useful when there are many small withdrawals from inventory on a regular basis, order costs are relatively small, it is desirable to group orders by supplier, or the buyer wants to take advantage of transportation economies from suppliers in the same area. Periodic systems can have negative effects as well. Lengthening the review period will result in greater inventory levels and a sudden change in demand can have disastrous results if safety stocks are not adequate. Another problem with periodic reviews is that if stock is not stored in its proper place because of poor housekeeping, the reviewer may order material that is not needed.

Fixed Order Quantity

If demand is constant, the periodic review model is the same as the instantaneous replenishment model discussed under order point systems. If demand is variable, the quantity to be ordered depends upon the replenishment lead time. The quantity to be ordered should be the average demand for the review period. The safety stock would be set based on the anticipated demand during the lead time as in the instantaneous replenishment model with uncertain demand.

Variable Order Quantity

The variable order quantity is based on a desired stock on hand. The desired stock on hand is the sum of the anticipated demand during the review period, the anticipated demand during the lead time, and the amount of safety stock desired. When the review period is reached, the amount ordered will be the desired stock level minus the stock on hand minus the stock on order but not received.

For example, given an anticipated demand of 143 units per week, a lead time of two weeks, a desired safety stock of 70 units, and a review period of three weeks, the desired stock level would be 785 units.

$$\begin{array}{c} (143 \text{ units/week})(2\text{-week lead time}) + (143 \text{ units/week}) \\ (3\text{-week review time}) + (70 \text{ units safety stock}) \end{array} \qquad (3.16)$$

If the current inventory is 350 units, the order quantity would be 435 units, 785 minus 350.

DISTRIBUTION SYSTEMS

Inventory in a distribution system can be managed through the use of independent demand models. The continuous and periodic review models developed earlier in the chapter can be applied in the distribution context. Additional models, such as double order point and sales replacement, have been developed that are based on the continuous and periodic review models but consider the unique problems caused by the multiple levels in the distribution chain.

One advantage of the distribution models is that they allow the various levels in the distribution chain to manage their inventories autonomously. Additionally, the models presented have relatively low data requirements, allowing them to be automated. The primary disadvantage of these models is that they ignore the other stages in the supply chain. The independent behavior can cause radical swings in demand at various stages in the chain, leading to stockouts and back orders. Additionally, excess shipping costs can be incurred since no one is coordinating the movement of materials within the system. A third problem is that demand for replenishment occurs without any regard for what is currently being produced or being planned to be produced in the production system. The need for an item may then incur extra setups, lost productivity, and excess transportation.

Order Point

The order point system is the application of any of the continuous review models in a distribution environment. The models basically ignore the fact that the order takes place in a chain and assumes that each element in the distribution system is independent of all other components. This independent behavior can cause large swings within the distribution system caused by a phenomenon called lumpy demand at the next level down in the distribution chain. For example, assume that a distributor serves 10 retailers, each with a uniform demand of 10 units per week and a fixed order quantity of 50 units. If the retailers' orders happen to coincide with each other, the distributor could experience four weeks with no demand followed by one week where orders for 500 units are received. Likewise, if a factory warehouse served 10 distributors who order 1,000 units at a time, the factory warehouse could experience weekly demands ranging from zero to 10,000 units. These large swings come from the lack of communication within the distribution system.

Periodic Review

In a periodic review system, orders are placed on a predetermined time schedule. The advantage is that the order times can be staggered throughout the chain to smooth the demand at each point in the distribution chain. This reduces peaks and valleys caused by several customers ordering at the same time. For example, in the previous example each of the 10 retailers could be assigned a specific week to place their orders, leveling the demand to the distributor at 100 units per week.

Double Order Point

The double order point system sets the reorder point based not only on the time it takes to get an order filled one level down in the distribution system but also on the lead time it takes the second level down to be replenished. For example, if a distributor is quoted a lead time from the factory warehouse of two weeks and it takes the factory warehouse three weeks to have stock replenished, the reorder point would be set based on the demand for a five-week period. The advantage is that it reduces the risk of material not being available, but it adds inventory to the safety stock to handle the increased possible exposure to a stockout.

Sales Replacement

Each stocking point in the distribution chain sets a desired stock level for each item on a regular basis. Then as sales take place they are reported back down the chain. When the regular replenishment time comes, the supplier ships only what the customer used or sold during the period. The objective of this system is to maintain a stable inventory level within the system and to pass the actual demand information down the system to avoid large fluctuations from period to period. This does require having enough inventory to cover the potential demand during the replenishment cycle, and information channels must be established. In essence, the sales replacement system is a periodic review model with variable order quantities.

KANBAN SYSTEMS

A popular type of inventory control system often discussed in conjunction with just-in-time (JIT) is the use of kanbans. Kanban, loosely translated, means "card" and is used to authorize the replacement of material as it is consumed. Kanbans are used in the JIT philosophy to control the flow of materials through the firm. In reality, kanbans are nothing more than a sales replacement system. They control inventory levels, primarily work-in-process, by allowing each operation to replace only what the next operation has used. The level of inventory is controlled by setting the number of kanbans to be used in a process. This system presupposes a relative uniform demand for items over time.

A kanban system consists of two parts: standard containers and production cards. The standard container is, in essence, a standard lot size since each container holds a specified number of items. Canon Inc., a manufacturer of

copies, cameras, and optical equipment, determines the number of containers for an item with the formula:

$$\text{Number of cards} = \frac{(PT + CT)\dfrac{(\text{Daily quantity})}{8}}{QH} \qquad (3.17)$$

where PT is processing time, which is the time needed to produce one container. CT is the conveyance cycle time, which is the time it takes to get
the item from one operation to the next, and QH is the quantity of parts
each standard container holds. The daily quantity is the amount of product
to be produced on a daily basis.[2] The daily quantity is divided by eight
hours per day to give the quantity needed hourly. With each container there
is also a production card that authorizes the supplying operation to produce one container of the item to replace the one just used. The same
effects can be accomplished using standard containers and designated
spaces for inventory.

The kanban system works best where there is a relatively smooth
flow in the operation and the demand is constant from day to day. It also
assumes that the process changeover times are relatively small, preferably
under ten minutes. In addition, kanbans are best applied when two operations are separated from each other such that one operation cannot see what
is going on in the other operation. The kanbans serve to prevent the buildup
of inventory if the customer process should slow down or stop or where the
supply process capacity exceeds the customer process usage. Another area
of application is when there is a significant difference in change over times
between successive operations. Kanbans serve to maintain the appropriate
inventory levels to keep the process running without creating excess. A
third application is when different work cells share a common piece of
equipment or work center. The kanbans serve to keep the volume of work
balanced with the supplying operations. A fourth application is to temporar-
ily decouple an operation that is having quality, capacity, or reliability problems. The kanban isolates the troublesome operation until the problem is

---

[2]Japan Management Association, *Canon Production System* (Stamford, Conn.: Productivity
Press, 1987), pp. 138–139.

[3]Edward J. Hay, *The Just-In-Time Breakthrough* (New York: John Wiley & Sons, Inc., 1988),
pp. 109–110.

resolved, at which time the kanbans are removed.[3] Removing a kanban is done by removing a container and its attendant production card from the production process.

PURCHASING'S ROLE

One would expect that with the proper application of the models discussed above, there should be few occasions of excess inventory or stockouts in the firm. However, a variety of circumstances can arise that cause problems with the models discussed in this chapter. There are at least four classes of problems that face any firm using independent demand models. They have to do with demand changes, cost changes, lead time changes, and quantity variations. The first class of problems occurs when demand increases or decreases or design changes take place. Demand increases usually cause continuous review models to order more frequently, increasing order costs, while periodic review models can experience shortages. Demand decreases commonly result in excess inventories in both continuous and periodic review models when order quantities are not reduced to reflect the lower demand. Design changes result in excess inventories, increasing carrying costs, especially obsolescence costs.

One implication for control is that the demand forecast used in any model needs to be regularly reviewed to ensure that the current demand estimate is compatible with the forecast used in developing the order quantity. A second implication is that purchasing (or production planning) needs to process requisitions in a timely fashion to reduce the risk of stockouts. Third, before ordering large quantities of an item, purchasing should check with engineering to determine the stability of the design to avoid committing the firm for material that may be declared obsolete.

A second class of problems comes from the cost information used in independent demand models. Price discounts, changing order costs, and minimum order quantities can all cause inventory problems. In the case of price discounts, the buyer should consider what effects the quantity required to obtain the discount will have on desired inventory performance measures, such as inventory turns, as well as the obsolescence risks. Purchasing can look at ways to improve its purchasing process to reduce the cost per order and cut down the purchasing administration element of lead time. The use of blanket orders, system contracts, or consignment inventories may lower order costs. Lower order costs lead to more frequent orders and lower inventory levels.

The third class of problems comes from lead time changes. Changing lead times affect reorder points and safety stocks. If the lead time increases, not only will the reorder point or base stock need to the increased, the level of safety stock required to maintain the desired service level will also increase. If those changes are not made, the risk of a stockout rises. If lead times decrease, reorder points and safety stocks can decrease or the firm will have excess inventory. As purchasing is the main contact with suppliers, it must maintain realistic lead time information that is promptly passed to the users and requisitioners. Also, purchasing needs to monitor supplier delivery performance, as early and late deliveries can both be expensive. Early delivery can lead to increased handling and damage costs as material has to be moved or is misplaced because the standard storage location is still full. Late deliveries lead to possible stockouts and shutdowns.

The last class of problems is quantity variations. Process yield rates and variations, supplier quality, and overshipments are all sources of quantity variations. Purchasing can work with suppliers to reduce process variations and increase quality levels. Reducing quantity variation helps reduce the level of safety stock needed to handle supply uncertainty. Overshipments are a small matter that on the surface appear to be insignificant but can result in excess inventories.

Accurate and timely information is critical to the usefulness of all the models discussed in this chapter. System training and discipline are essential. The problem in many companies is that models are often installed, calculations made, and decisions implemented over time without review of the basic data—order costs, carrying costs, lead times, and demand. Purchasing has a responsibility to verify, maintain, and disseminate accurate information about its supply processes and environment.

CHAPTER SUMMARY

This chapter has presented a number of models for managing independent demand inventories. Key points are:

- In general, independent demand inventory systems are pull systems, replacing what a successive operation or customer has consumed.
- Continuous review systems monitor the level of inventory every time an inventory transaction takes place and determine if a replenishment order needs to be made.

- Continuous review systems include fixed order quantity and variable order quantity models.
- Fixed order quantity models include the instantaneous replenishment, noninstantaneous replenishment, price discount, and instantaneous replenishment with uncertain demand.
- Periodic review systems check inventory levels on a periodic basis as opposed to a transaction basis.
- Periodic review systems can have both fixed and variable order quantities.
- Distribution systems include order point, periodic review, double order point, and sales replacement models.
- Kanban systems, normally seen in conjunction with JIT, use a fixed order quantity, sales replacement system, primarily for controlling work-in-process inventories.
- Managing independent demand inventory systems means dealing with the problems caused by changes in demand, lead times, costs, and quantities.
- Purchasing can help manage independent demand inventories by reviewing the planning parameters for changes before placing an order, determining if any design changes are in process or planned for the near future, verifying lead time estimates, and evaluating the order quantity relative to the recent demand and the desired performance inventory measures.

REFERENCES

Fogarty, Donald W., Thomas R. Hoffman, and Peter W. Stonebraker. *Production and Operations Management.* Cincinnati, Ohio: South-Western Publishing Co., 1989.

Hall, Robert W. *Attaining Manufacturing Excellence.* Homewood, Ill.: Dow Jones-Irwin, 1987.

Hay, Edward J. *The Just-In-Time Breakthrough.* New York: John Wiley & Sons, Inc., 1988.

Japan Management Association. *The Canon Production System.* Stamford, Conn.: Productivity Press, 1987.

Plossl, George W. *Production and Inventory Control: Principles and Techniques,* 2nd ed. Englewood Cliffs, N.J.: Prentice Hall, Inc., 1985.

Vollmann, Thomas E., William L. Berry, and D. Clay Whybark. *Manufacturing Planning and Control Systems,* 3rd ed. Homewood, Ill.: Irwin, 1992.

CHAPTER 4

MANAGING DEPENDENT DEMAND SYSTEMS

INTRODUCTION

In Chapter 3 we used the analogy of a drive up Pike's Peak with a modified car to illustrate how a reorder point system functions. Our car had a windshield that was painted black, the windows and sunroof were sealed shut, and the transmission was locked in drive. We could react only as we passed major events on the road. Using the same analogy under the dependent demand concept, we again will venture up the mountain but in a normal vehicle. The road is sometimes clearly seen, sometimes clouds or fog set in to obscure our vision, but the point is that we are able to see what is happening in front of us rather than what happened in the past. The dependent demand principle is not directly an inventory management concept but rather is based on understanding the supply processes and planning accordingly. Inventory is controlled by managing the planning process.

This chapter begins with a discussion of material requirements planning, its benefits, the requirements for a successful implementation, how an MRP system generates planned orders, and the classes of MRP systems. Capacity requirements planning is discussed next, followed by a look at the issues involved in effectively implementing a successful MRP/MRP II system. The chapter concludes with a look at distribution requirements planning and purchasing's involvement with MRP.

MATERIAL REQUIREMENTS PLANNING

Material requirements planning (MRP) is not a new concept. What has made the process feasible today is the widespread use of the computer. In an organization with 10,000 part numbers, it simply was not possible to plan the usage of each item on a timely basis manually. As with all great concepts, this concept is elegant in its simplicity but difficult to bring about. Simply stated, an MRP system says, "Tell me what needs to done tomorrow and I'll tell you what actions need to be taken today to make tomorrow happen."

The objectives of the MRP system are (1) to determine what, how much, and when to order and when to schedule delivery, and (2) to keep priorities current for inventory planning, capacity requirements planning, and shop floor control. By planning production of the end items and knowing what materials are on hand and are required to produce the end item, the MRP system can determine what needs to be purchased or produced to allow the end item to be produced on time. For example, if a company plans to produce 100 automobiles next week and it takes one week to obtain steering wheels, 100 steering wheels need to be ordered this week so that the cars can be assembled on schedule. The second part of the MRP system is that it keeps track of the flow of materials through the firm. This information is used to keep job priorities up to date and to anticipate capacity needs, both equipment and labor, in the future.

The potential benefits of an MRP system are many. The key thing to keep in mind with these benefits is that they come simply from doing a better job of managing the planning process. These benefits are exclusive of any changes made to improve the production or supply processes.

Lower inventories.   Inventories are reduced by better planning. Because materials are scheduled based on planned usage, the need for safety stocks and excess inventories is reduced, especially work-in-process inventories. For example, Mentor Graphics, a manufacturer of computer-aided design and computer-aided engineering systems, saw an increase in inventory turns from 2 to 7 in a three-year period through the use of MRP.

Better customer service.   Customer service benefits in several ways. First, better planning reduces throughput times thus reducing lead times. One company, when implementing an MRP system, discovered that their actual lead times were 12 weeks even though they were quoting the industry standard of delivery in six weeks. When they approached their customers to let them know they were aware of the problem, the customers were not surprised. A year later when the company began delivering in six weeks, there was a mad scramble by customers to readjust their orders, since they had been ordering based on a 12-week delivery time.

A second benefit is a reduction in split orders. Split orders occur when production or delivery of a customer's order is split into two or more parts because of a lack of materials. At best it means an extra setup and at worst could cause a late or partial shipment to the customer. Mentor Graphics discovered that order/delivery accuracy went from 60 percent to 99 percent in a three-year period and on-time shipments improved from 50 percent to 90 percent in the same period. This also resulted in a reduction of the accounts receivables from 80 days to 60 days. As errors were reduced, billing disputes declined, leading to lower receivables.

Better scheduling.   Better scheduling is possible as the MRP systems allows more effective expediting and better use of capacity. If the MRP system is working properly, one of the benefits is up-to-date information on the status of every order within the company. Since the MRP system models the relationships between items, when a due date changes on one item, the due dates on other items that are affected can be updated, reducing the "hurry up and wait" syndrome common in many organizations. Additionally, because needs are being planned up to a year in advance, the MRP system can identify short-term capacity problems and allow planners to move orders forward or backward in time to alleviate potential problems. Mentor Graphics saw their output per work week double in a three–year period with little to no change in manpower.

Early warning system for delivery.   By having a time horizon of up to a year in the future, capacity and supply problems can be anticipated. Many companies provide their suppliers weekly printouts of key items from the MRP system. This, at a minimum, allows the supplier to anticipate increases or decreases in needs on a more timely basis. Some companies even use the MRP report as an order release mechanism.

Long–range planning.   Because the MRP system is planning up to a year in advance, it can provide a tool to aid management in identifying the needs of the organization in terms of equipment and labor by work center. It can also serve as a modeling tool to identify the effects of process changes on inventories and deliveries and to model the financial state of the organization.

Requirements for MRP

The five basic prerequisites for the successful implementation of an MRP system are a feasible master schedule, accurate inventory records, accurate bills of materials (BOMs), known lead times, and unique part numbers. The paradox to implementing an MRP system is that probably half of the benefits of an MRP system come from meeting these basic requirements, yet most firms do not have these requirements in place. They are looking for the MRP system to provide the motivation, structure, and discipline to allow them to meet these requirements. Let's look at what each of these requirements entails.

Feasible Master Schedule

The master production schedule (MPS) is the plan of what is to be produced by time period. This schedule is stated in terms of end items, which could be shippable products or highest level subassemblies. For example, a large truck manufacturer uses the MPS to schedule major subassemblies such as heaters and engines on several product lines with limited options. The customer is allowed to custom design a particular model within a narrow set of options. Thus the final assembly is to customer order but the production of the major subassemblies is based upon the MPS. This allows the firm to have long lead time items available even when the exact product mix is unknown.

The MPS is based upon confirmed orders, interplant orders, forecast sales (including service part requirements), current inventory levels, lead times (both internal and supplier), and capacity levels. The old adage, "Plan your work and work your plan," applies here. The result is a plan of end item production that cascades into the needs for all subassemblies, components, and raw materials.

The planning horizon for the MPS should be at least equal to the longest cumulative procurement and manufacturing lead time for an end item. The normal time frame for an MPS is at least one year. The exact breakdown of the time buckets does vary from firm to firm. Within the planning horizon many firms have a practice of freezing a portion of the MPS to prevent changes in the MPS to which the manufacturing operations cannot react in a timely and economical fashion. For example, one equipment manufacturer has divided the master schedule into four segments. The schedule for the first four weeks is not subject to change, and suppliers are guaranteed that the firm will acquire the indicated quantities and will pay for them. The second four weeks are guaranteed plus or minus 10 percent and the third four weeks plus or minus 25 percent. All needs beyond three months are for the supplier's information and are subject to change.

There are three assumptions regarding the master production schedule. First, the MPS exists. Second, the MPS is stated in terms of the end items or subassemblies as specified in the bill of materials. Third, the resulting schedule is feasible in terms of material availability, labor capacity, and machine capacity.

Accurate Inventory Records

Accurate inventory records are necessary to determine the appropriate quantity and timing of each item to order or manufacture. The MRP system cannot make the proper recommendations for action with wrong information. The normal requirement is for at least 95 percent accuracy. The definition of accurate depends on the individual firm and the item itself. For example, finished goods may require exact quantities, while bulk items or extremely small or hard-to-count items could be within $100 in value. Cycle counting is generally used to maintain the required inventory accuracy.

The data requirements for the inventory module can be partitioned into three types: master data, status data, and support status data. Master data consist of the general information about an item such as part number, description, classification, cost, order quantity, lead time, scrap allowance, and safety stock. Status data include information on current inventory levels, on-hand and allocated, and order information such as scheduled receipts and past due information. Support status data include open order information, historical usage and lead time data, and scrap information.

Accurate Bill of Materials

The bill of materials (BOM) tells the MRP system what items are used to produce the finished product or subassembly. The minimum requirement is 95 percent accuracy. If the BOM does not accurately reflect what is required to build the product, the results can be catastrophic.

For example, assume a firm builds upholstered chairs. An order is received to manufacture 100 units of model R. The assembly department supervisor sends out an order picker to obtain all the necessary components. All goes fine until the order picker returns and says, "I can't find the XYZs." The supervisor checks the inventory report, which indicates there are 139 on hand, and sends the order picker out again to find the XYZs.

After the employee returns empty-handed a second time, the supervisor says, "Tell you what, bring me 100 GHIs. They can substitute for XYZs and we have to get this order out this week." So the order is shipped using 100 GHIs. The next week, assembly gets an order for 75 of model U, which uses part GHI. Now the order picker returns and says, "I can find only 25 GHIs but the inventory report says we have 125 on hand. However, I did find those XYZs we were looking for last week." The supervisor, realizing what went wrong, says, "That's great, except XYZs cannot substitute for GHIs. I'd better call up fabrication and get a rush order started for GHIs if we are going to get this order out."

The MRP system uses the bill of materials to determine what material is needed and when. It is used to automatically reduce the inventory of all components and raw materials as product is completed. In the example above, the system thought that at the end of the first week there were 39 XYZs and 125 GHIs left when in reality there were 139 XYZs and 25 GHIs remaining. Because the actions on the shop floor did not reflect the planning information in the MRP system, the integrity of the system had been compromised. Additionally, close control of the BOM is necessary to prevent obsolete inventory caused by design changes and to ensure that the right components and materials are ordered.

Bills of materials can take a variety of forms—level of manufacturing bills, phantom bills, pseudo bills, modular bills, and where used bills. Let's look at each type briefly by examining the manufacture and assembly of a ballpoint pen.

Levels of manufacturing. Level of manufacturing bills reflect the way material flows in and out of stages of completion. The BOM specifies not only the composition of the product but the process stages in the product's manufacture. These bills can be presented in several forms. The

TABLE 4.1
Example Single Level Final Assembly Bill of Materials

Part No.	Description	Quantity Required	Unit of Measure
PB001W	Pen barrel, white	1	Each
IC010B	Ink cartridge, blue	1	Each
SP231	Spring, 1"	1	Each
PT320R	Pen cap assembly, red	1	Each

TABLE 4.2
Example Indented Bill of Materials

Part No.	Description	Quantity Required	Unit of Measure
PB001W	Pen barrel, white	1	Each
PL438W	Plastic beads, white	4	Ounces
IC010B	Ink cartridge, blue	1	Each
SP231	Spring, 1"	1	Each
PT320R	Pen cap subassembly, red	1	Each
PC034	Pen cap, red	1	Each
PL438R	Plastic beads, red	3	Ounces
CP845	Pocket clip	1	Each
ST839	Steel strip, 1/4" by 1.5"	1	Each
PA754	Plunger subassembly	1	Each
PC593	Plunger cap, metal	1	Each
PC437	Plunger top, plastic	1	Each
PL438W	Plastic beads, white	2	Ounces
PC436	Plunger base, plastic	1	Each
PL438B	Plastic beads, blue	1	Ounce

single level bill (Table 4.1) lists the materials required for final assembly of an end item. This includes the part numbers, part descriptions, quantity required, and the part units of measure. The part units of measure indicates the unit of measure of the item as it is used in the product as distinguished from the unit of measure used in purchasing the item. For example, the purchase unit of measure for an item might be 100-pound bags while the production unit of measure is pounds. Table 4.2 presents the same information again in a multiple level, indented bill form where each level of indentation indicates the level the item is in the tree. Figure 4.1 presents the same information in a tree form where the end item is considered level zero.

Phantom bills.   Phantom bills, also called transient subassemblies or phantom parts, are bills of material that include items which normally do not go into inventory. This allows the combining of common parts to reduce the number of items in the BOM. For example, in Table 4.2 the pen cap subassembly and plunger subassembly are phantom parts. They should never be stored in inventory but are convenient planning tools, as the pen barrels might vary with a customer's logo while the tops remain the same.

FIGURE 4.1
Example Bill of Materials Tree

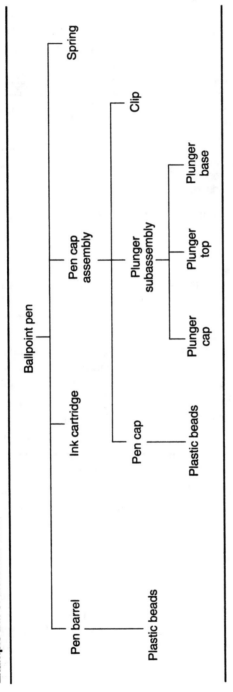

Modular bills.   Modular bills are used to create pseudo subassemblies for which components are split based on the percentage makeup in the total order. They are used primarily to disentangle combinations of optional product features and to segregate common from unique parts. For example, using the BOM in Table 4.1, the demand for the ink cartridges could be blue 37 percent of the time and black the remaining 63 percent of the time. This allows the planner to schedule just one model of pen but results in purchasing ordering the required number of blue and black ink cartridges.

Planning bills.   Also called pseudo bills, super bills, or family bills, planning bills are used to plan at an even higher level than modular bills. A planning bill could be used to plan a whole family of pens including custom and standard. A second type of planning bill is the bill of labor, which relates the labor requirements to each item in the BOM.

Where used (implosion) bills.   The where used bill specifies all the parents of a particular part—that is, every place the subject part is used. Using the example in Table 4.2, part number PL438W would show PB001W and PC437 as parents. An implosion bill is useful when problems such as supplier quality or delivery occur. The implosion bill will show, across product lines, which parts and products will be affected by the problem.

Known Lead Times

After the MRP logic determines when each item is required, it calculates when to order the item based upon the lead time to purchase or manufacture the part. Thus the MRP system requires a lead time estimate for every part number in the system. This applies to all parts, internally or externally supplied. Without realistic lead time information, the purchase timing recommendations made by the MRP system will be worthless. Since lead times are dynamic, changing with business conditions, it is essential that they be updated promptly.

Unique Part Numbers

This requirement always sounds too simple to be important, yet often organizations have problems with part numbers. A pump manufacturer regularly refers to modified parts for a customer order by the standard part number, causing needless confusion in planning. The MRP system requires that each different part be identified with a unique part number no matter where it is used in the organization. This can be a problem in multiple divisions sharing a common database where each division has its own unique part number for the identical part.

Generating Planned Order Releases

The MRP system begins with a feasible master schedule for each end item and a bill of materials and beginning inventory information for each part; from that information, it generates a planned order release for each item. Let us use the ballpoint pen example shown in Figure 4.1. Figure 4.2 shows the generation of the planned order releases for ballpoint pen assembly, pen cap assembly, and pen cap production. We will assume that there are 370 completed pens, 60 pen cap assemblies, and 70 pen caps in inventory. The pens may be sold the same week that they are produced (lead time = zero). The lead times for pen cap assemblies and pen caps are both one week. There are also orders in process that were generated in week zero for 110 pen cap assemblies and 380 pen caps to be delivered in week one.

The MPS for ballpoint pens becomes the gross requirements for the ballpoint pen assembly. The on-hand inventory for a week is calculated by adding the on-hand inventory from the previous week plus the scheduled receipts for the week and subtracting the gross requirements for the week. If the result is positive, the number goes into the on-hand inventory cell for the week. If the result is negative, the absolute value of the number goes into the net requirements cell for the week. A negative on-hand inventory is a positive requirement. For week 1, the on-hand inventory for the previous week is 370, there are no scheduled receipts, and the gross requirement is 500. The result is −130 (370 + 0 − 500 = −130); therefore, 130 goes into the net requirements cell. For week 2, there are no on-hand inventory and no scheduled receipts; therefore, the gross requirement becomes the net requirement. In fact, once the initial on-hand inventory and the previously scheduled receipts are netted out, the gross requirements become the net requirements. Since the lead time for ballpoint pen assembly is zero weeks, the net requirement becomes the planned order release. In other words, the MRP system is telling the Ballpoint Pen Assembly Department to assemble 130 pens in week 1 and to plan on producing 430 pens in week 2.

FIGURE 4.2
MRP Calculations Example

Week	1	2	3	4	5	6	7	8
Master production schedule	500	430	680	525	300	0	245	320

Ballpoint pen assembly

		1	2	3	4	5	6	7	8
Gross requirements		500	430	680	525	300	0	245	320
On-hand inventory	370								
Scheduled receipts									
Net requirements		130	430	680	525	300	0	245	320
Planned order releases		130	430	680	525	300	0	245	320

Pen cap assembly

		1	2	3	4	5	6	7	8
Gross requirements		130	430	680	525	300	0	245	320
On-hand inventory	60	40							
Scheduled receipts		110							
Net requirements		0	390	680	525	300	0	245	320
Planned order releases		390	680	525	300	0	245	320	—

Pen cap

		1	2	3	4	5	6	7	8
Gross requirements		390	680	525	300	0	245	320	—
On-hand inventory	70	60							
Scheduled receipts		380							
Net requirements		0	620	525	300	0	245	320	—
Planned order releases		620	525	300	245	320	—	—	—

The planned order releases for the parent become the gross requirements for the child in the bill of materials. Since the pen cap assembly is the child of (goes into) the ballpoint pen assembly, the planned production for the ballpoint pens will determine the demand for pen cap assemblies. Thus the gross requirements for the pen cap assemblies match the planned order releases for the ballpoint pen assembly. The process of determining the net requirements is the same for each component in the bill of materials. Since the pen cap assemblies take one week to be manufactured, the planned order releases need to be offset by one week so that the completed assemblies arrive on time. Continuing the example, in order to receive 390 pen cap assemblies in week 2, they must be ordered in week 1. The process of moving the net requirements back the number of periods equal to the lead time is called time-phasing. The pen cap goes through the same process as the pen cap assembly, offsetting order dates by the length of the lead time.

The process used to determine the planned order release in the example is called lot-for-lot lot sizing. There are a number of other methods for lot sizing, such as periodic order quantity, least total cost, and part-period balancing. The object of these alternate lot sizing methods is to minimize the ordering and carrying costs.

Classes of MRP

The basic components just described make up what is often called a Class C MRP system. The lightly shaded area in Figure 4.3 illustrates the basic Class C system. This is often called an open system since there is no formal feedback loop to the master scheduling process. The outputs of this system consist of the planned purchases and the planned production order releases.

When a shop floor control module, which includes information about how each part is manufactured, process routes, and times, is added to the process, there is now the capability to begin to estimate capacity loads. A capacity requirements planning module takes the inputs from the shop floor control module and sums the loads on each work center to develop a capacity load for each work center for each time period. This information can be fed into the master scheduling and shop floor control processes to reduce bottlenecks and anticipate future problems. The dark shaded area in Figure 4.3 shows a Class B MRP system.

FIGURE 4.3
Class C Through Class A MRP System

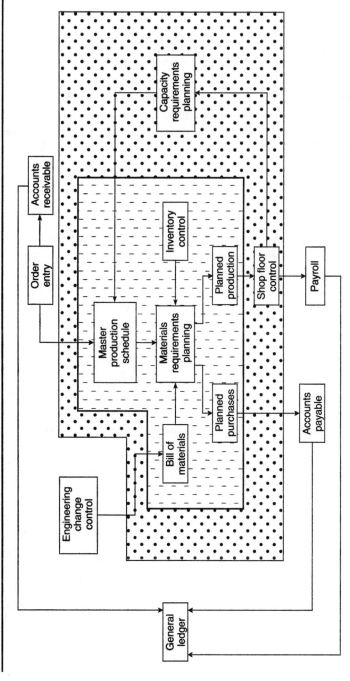

The addition of several additional modules outside the shaded areas shown in Figure 4.3 creates what is commonly called a Class A MRP system or MRP II, which stands for the second definition of MRP, manufacturing resource planning. Additional modules include order entry, engineering changes, accounts payable, payroll, accounts receivable, and general ledger, which create a complete financial model of the manufacturing firm driven by the production plan. Planners and managers can simulate the effects of various scheduling decisions on the firm looking at both short-term and medium-range effects.

CAPACITY REQUIREMENTS PLANNING

Capacity requirements planning (CRP) is the process of establishing, measuring, and adjusting the levels of capacity within the firm. This includes determining both labor and equipment resources necessary to meet the master production schedule. CRP manages the capacity by beginning the processing of an order early, finding alternative routings, using overtime, and, as a last resort, modifying the master production schedule.

The CRP system takes planned order releases from the MRP system for production items and feeds them into a shop floor control system. The shop floor control system schedules the routing of each item through the production process, including lead time offsets. The CRP system aggregates the production plan by summing the planned workloads for all items by work center and time period. This workload is then compared to the available labor and equipment capacity by work center. Adjustments can then be made to order releases to bring capacity requirements and production schedules in line with available capacity.

There are two approaches to developing a schedule in CRP. Backward scheduling determines the release date for an order by working backward from the planned due date or scheduled completion date. Forward scheduling begins at the planned release date and works forward to determine the planned due date.

If the scheduling is done without regard to other jobs already scheduled at each work center, it is called infinite loading. If the scheduling process is performed using priorities for each order and considering the available capacity at each work center, it is called finite loading. Finite loading has the drawback of not presenting a picture of where and when capacity problems exist. Infinite loading ignores the realities of capacity limitations. The best approach is iterative. First, schedule using infinite loading to identify bottlenecks. After taking steps to reduce the bottlenecks, use finite loading to determine the best schedule within the capacity limitations.

ATTAINING MRP II

Many issues are involved in effectively implementing a complex system such as MRP and MRP II. The issues can be categorized into five areas: goal setting, top management support, implementation process, technical issues, and project evaluation.

Goal Setting
Probably one of the most important issues is the establishment of realistic goals for the MRP system. However, before a firm can effectively set targets, it must first measure the current performance levels for the measures it selects. Appropriate measures might include inventory accuracy, bill of material accuracy, on-time shipment performance, number of split orders, inventory turns, and process lead times. Without starting values for these measures, the firm will have a difficult time determining the effectiveness of the MRP implementation.

Top Management Support
As with all major projects, without top management support and commitment, the MRP implementation is destined for failure. The implementation of an MRP system is a journey, not a destination. It takes a number of years to move from no system to a smoothly running MRP II system. The implementation process requires changes in policies, procedures, organization, and employee time. Management must be willing to commit the necessary resources in order to make the project successful. This is why measuring the beginning level of performance is so important. As long as management can look back and see the progress over time and forward to the target, it becomes much easier to provide consistent support.

Implementation Process
The implementation process is also an important consideration. One factor is the selection of the project team. The team should consist of individuals from a wide range of areas within the firm including purchasing,

production planning, accounting, sales, engineering, shipping and receiving, a variety of production departments, and data processing. The diversity of the team serves two functions. The first is to provide the unique perspectives that each area brings to the production control and planning process. Second, the diversity of the team helps the assimilation process as changes are implemented.

A second factor in the implementation process is education. The implementation of an MRP system requires major changes in responsibility for everyone within the firm. Without education about what MRP is, how it works, and the importance of accurate information at all times, the project is doomed to failure. Training should cover everyone in the firm, and include hands-on experience in running the specific software the firm will be using. This process should start early and continue beyond startup.

A third factor in the implementation process is phased implementation. The preferred process is to move through the implementation one step at a time. It probably is better to begin by using the inventory and bill of material modules first as data accuracy is built up. Often if a product line or business unit is relatively self-contained, the implementation process can start in that one area. As that area comes on line, other product lines or business units can be added.

Technical Issues

A fourth area is technical issues. These are concerned with software selection, hardware, and data accuracy. Software selection is a major concern. There are many good packages available. One of the best checklists I have seen was published in *Datamation* in 1983[1] listing the factors Lexitron used in the selection of an MRP system. The first step would be to review the Lexitron specification for items that are not relevant to a company's needs and for issues that are not included. Given the specification, software packages would then be evaluated. A good rule of thumb is that if the package meets 80 to 90 percent of the firm's needs, it should be considered. The biggest mistake a firm can make is to quickly select a piece of software and then begin modifying it. This will delay the implementation and when problems do occur will result in lots of finger pointing before the issue is resolved. The firm is better off to change its control processes to fit the software unless something in the process results in a competitive

---

[1]"Lexitron's Functional Specification for MRP Software," *Datamation,* January 1983, pp. 90–98.

advantage to the firm. Hardware problems generally revolve around an adequate number of terminals throughout the firm giving timely access to all who need it. Data accuracy is critical for the system's success. Developing the discipline throughout the firm to maintain up-to-date information should be a key focal point of the education process.

Evaluation Process

The evaluation process is important in determining the project's advancement toward the original targets. This provides feedback to all concerned about improvements to date and areas that will need further attention. The Oliver Wight company publishes a checklist that can be used to evaluate the performance of the firm's entire production planning and control process.[2]

DISTRIBUTION REQUIREMENTS PLANNING

Distribution requirements planning (DRP) and distribution resource planning (DRP II) are applications of the time-phasing logic of MRP to the distribution function. Figure 4.4 shows the structure of the DRP system. Viewing the MRP system as the root structure of the end item, DRP is the branches as they come out from the trunk. The purpose of DRP is to forecast the demand by distribution center to determine the master scheduling needs. As opposed to the order point based distribution systems discussed in Chapter 3, DRP attempts to anticipate the future needs throughout the distribution chain and plan deliveries accordingly.

PURCHASING'S INVOLVEMENT WITH MRP

Purchasing is involved with MRP in two ways. The first is as a provider of information and the second is as a user of the MRP system. Since the success of an MRP system is dependent on the quality of information within the system, purchasing has a major responsibility for providing good lead time information. Purchasing also has a responsibility to update delivery information as it becomes available to keep the planning information current and allow for changes in priorities when material is not available as scheduled.

---

[2]*The Oliver Wight ABCD Checklist for Operational Excellence,* 4th ed. (Essex Junction, Vt.: Oliver Wight, 1992).

FIGURE 4.4
Example Distribution Requirements Planning System

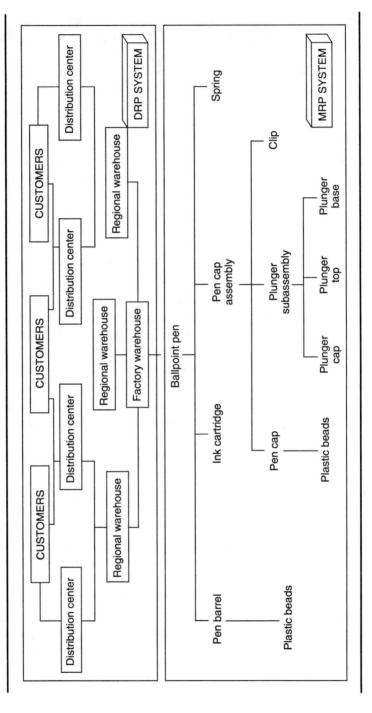

The ability of the MRP system to provide planning information by product for future periods has great benefit to purchasing. Negotiations can be conducted with suppliers for longer term contracts based on anticipated volumes from a production plan. Additionally, supplier relations can be improved as the planning information improves, since the supplier knows what will be required in the future. Order releases can replace purchase orders, thus freeing purchasing to spend more time on supplier development, new product development, and supplier certification. Purchasing can focus on developing capacity needs with suppliers to help reduce product lead time.

CHAPTER SUMMARY

This chapter has looked at material requirements planning, its components and implementation. Key points are:

- The benefits of MRP accrue through improved management of the planning process, not through process improvement.
- Benefits of MRP include lower inventories, better customer service, better scheduling, early warning system for deliveries, and improved long-range planning.
- The requirements for a successful MRP implementation are a feasible master schedule, accurate inventory records, accurate bills of materials, known lead times, and unique part numbers.
- The implementation of material requirements planning concepts progresses through three stages. The first, called Class C, is the basic open-ended MRP system. The addition of shop floor control and capacity requirements planning, closing the control loop, brings the implementation to Class B. Class A, or manufacturing resource planning (MRP II), brings the remainder of the firm's planning processes, as well as the accounting information, into the planning system.
- Capacity requirements planning uses the product routing information to establish the demand on each work center in order to allow rescheduling, use of alternative routings or overtime, or, if necessary, modification of the master schedule to reduce or avoid capacity problems.
- Successful implementation of an MRP II system is dependent on five areas: goal setting, top management support, implementation process, technical issues, and project evaluation.

- Distribution requirements planning (DRP) and distribution resource planning (DRP II) are the application of the time phasing logic of MRP to the distribution system. DRP uses forecasts and known order patterns from customers in the distribution chain to develop the demand on the master schedule.
- Purchasing is involved in MRP as both an information provider and user. Purchasing has responsibility for updating lead time information and order status. MRP also frees purchasing from order placing tasks to allow more time for supplier development, new product development, and supplier certification.

REFERENCES

Blackstone, Jr., John H. *Capacity Management.* Cincinnati, Ohio: South-Western Publishing Co., 1989.

Lunn, Terry, with Susan A. Neff. *MRP: Integrating Material Requirements Planning and Modern Business.* Homewood, Ill.: Business One Irwin, 1992.

Martin, Andre J. *DRP Distribution Resource Planning.* Essex Junction, Vt.: Oliver Wight Limited Publications, Inc., 1983.

Vollmann, Thomas E., William L. Berry, and D. Clay Whybark. *Manufacturing Planning and Control Systems,* 3rd ed. Homewood, Ill.: Irwin, 1992.

SECTION 3

MATERIAL FLOW

CHAPTER 5

INBOUND LOGISTICS

INTRODUCTION

A definite trend exists for purchasing to become more involved in making freight carrier decisions and in managing inbound freight. A 1991 Center for Advanced Purchasing Studies report indicated that:

- 91 percent of respondents were involved in inbound transportation decisions,
- 85 percent were involved in selecting inbound carriers,
- Over 40 percent had increased their level of inbound involvement in the last three years, and
- Over 57 percent of the purchase transactions of the respondents were F.O.B. origin.[1]

This chapter deals with managing inbound logistics. Topics include packaging, a review of transportation basics, carrier selection and contracting, and the receiving process. Strategies for the use of JIT principles in transportation, such as pooling inbound loads to reduce order size while gaining full load economies, will be discussed. The areas of special concern to purchasing will be highlighted.

TRANSPORTATION

With the increasing involvement of purchasing in inbound logistics, the purchaser needs to understand the basics of the transportation system in the United States. First, this section will look at the various modes of

---

[1]Julie J. Gentry, *Purchasing's Involvement in Transportation Decision Making* (Tempe, Ariz.: Center for Advanced Purchasing Studies/National Association of Purchasing Management, 1991).

transportation followed by the types of carriers and an overview of transportation regulations. Next, it will discuss freight rates and documentation followed by factors to consider in selecting a carrier. Last will be a discussion of transportation control and consolidation.

Modes of Transportation

The primary modes of freight transportation are water, motor carrier, rail, air, and pipeline. Two other forms of transportation are intermodal combinations and nonshippers. A brief overview of each mode follows.

Water
Water transportation includes inland, coastal, intercoastal, and international deep sea shipping. Inland waterways are navigable waters such as the Mississippi River, St. Lawrence Seaway, and Columbia River. It is the least costly and slowest form of shipping and used mainly for high-bulk, low-value products such as grain, ores, or petroleum. Coastal water shipments move between ports on one U.S. coast, while intercoastal shipping is between different coasts, that is, east coast to west coast. International deep sea shipping is between different countries. Water transportation is usually considered to be low in cost, slow in speed, somewhat inconsistent in delivery time, and low in damage. It is limited in access and requires the use of some other mode of transportation to get the product from inland source to inland destination. Inland waterways handled about 16 percent of the intercity freight in the United States in 1990.[2]

Motor Carrier
Motor carrier, or trucking, is the most commonly used form of transportation for moving quantities of materials under 30,000 to 40,000 pounds. It is competitive with air under 500 miles on service and cost and can compete with rail in truckload quantities up to 100,000 pounds over any distance. Its advantages include flexibility, ability to go practically anywhere a road exists, low damage, and relatively low delivery time variation. Its primary disadvantage is the load limitations of size and total weight. In

---

[2]Douglas M. Lambert and James R. Stock, *Strategic Logistics Management,* 3rd ed. (Homewood, Ill.: Irwin, 1993), p. 175.

1990, motor carriers accounted for approximately 26 percent of the ton-miles of intercity freight in the United States.[3]

Air

Air freight, due to its relatively high cost, is generally viewed as a premium form of transportation to be used for high-value, low-bulk goods. It is also used for emergency purposes. As with water, it moves product only from terminal to terminal and must rely on another mode, usually motor carrier, to move the product to its final destination. It is fast and reliable and has a low loss and damage level. Because of terminal time and pickup and delivery, it is faster than truck only above the 400-to 500-mile range.

Rail

Rail is the second slowest mode of transportation and is used primarily for low-value commodity items. Unless a company has a rail siding, rail provides only terminal-to-terminal service, thus relying on motor carrier to move the product to its final destination. It tends to have the highest damage level of any of the modes of transportation because of the large shocks received every time the train stops or starts.

Pipeline

Pipelines accounted for 20 percent of the intercity freight ton-miles in 1990. A majority of the material transported by pipeline is natural gas and crude oil. Pipelines have a low unit transportation cost, are highly dependable, and have low damage and loss rates. They are limited to items that can be moved in a liquid, gas, or slurry form.

Intermodal Combinations

There are several intermodal combinations based on the concept of piggybacking. Piggybacking in rail or water involves the use of a container that is designed to be moved on a flatcar or ship that can then be set on a trailer chassis and hauled by truck to the final destination point. The advantages of the concept are that the material being transported needs to be loaded and unloaded only once and the transportation costs are reduced by using a lower cost mode of transportation for the majority of the distance moved. A similar

---

[3]Lambert and Stock, p. 175.

concept is called roadrailer, where both rail wheels and rubber truck tires are mounted on the trailer. When the unit is used on a train, the rail wheels are used and the rubber tires are retracted. For highway use, the rail wheels are retracted and the rubber tires are used. This reduces the loading and unloading time of the piggyback method.

Nonshippers

Nonshippers are third parties that act as intermediaries in the transportation process. Freight forwarders purchase transportation services from the standard transportation modes in large quantities. They then consolidate the smaller shipments from a number of shippers into a larger load. Thus the freight forwarder purchases transportation at truckload or carload rates and then sells the space to smaller shippers at a rate that is lower than less-than-truckload or less-than-carload rates but higher than truckload or carload rates.

Shipper associations are nonprofit cooperatives that consolidate small shipments into larger shipments for the benefit of its members. They function similar to a freight forwarder but are not subject to Interstate Commerce Commission regulation.

A third form of nonshipper is the broker. The broker arranges for the transportation of products and charges a fee for the service. The broker can serve as a traffic department for the small-to medium-sized firm or can act as an agent in seeing that an organization's private fleet is used effectively.

Carrier Types

Among the various transportation modes, there are several types of carriers. The standard carrier types are common, contract, exempt, and private.

Common Carriers

Common carriers provide service to any shipper between two or more points at a published rate. They are granted authority to operate by the federal government, which specifies the commodities that can be carried and the markets the carrier can serve. "A common carrier is required to publish its rates, supply adequate facilities, provide service to all points prescribed in its certificate of authority, deliver the goods entrusted to its care within a reasonable time, charge reasonable rates, and refrain from discrimination against customers."[4]

------

[4]Lambert and Stock, p. 188.

Contract Carriers

A contract carrier is a for-hire carrier that does not purport to serve the general public but serves a set of shippers on a contractual basis. The carrier is still required to have an operating authority from the federal government to carry the relevant commodities in the required areas.

Exempt Carriers

An exempt carrier is a contract carrier that is not limited to routes, area served, or rates. The exemption is based on the commodity carried and the nature of the operation. The classification originally came out of the agricultural sector to allow farmers to move their products to market using public roads. Exemption also applies to local cartage firms operating within a municipal area.

Private Carriers

Private carriers are not for hire and are not subject to economic regulation. One example is a company's private fleet; for example, Fred Meyer, a Pacific Northwest retailer, uses its own trucks to supply its stores throughout the region. The deregulation of the trucking industry in 1980 now allows private carriers to operate as for-hire carriers for the purpose of securing backhaul loads from nonaffiliated companies.

Transportation Regulation

The major federal agencies that regulate transportation are the Interstate Commerce Commission (ICC), Department of Transportation (DOT), Federal Maritime Commission (FMC), and Federal Energy Regulatory Commission (FERC). All carriers are subject to safety, environmental, size, weight, and vehicle condition regulations. The DOT regulates safety for all modes and the economics of air carriers. The other agencies regulate the economic aspects of the other modes. A discussion of the transportation regulations could fill several tomes. The purpose here will be to present briefly the changes brought about by deregulation and their implications for the purchaser or materials manager.

Motor Carrier Act of 1980

One of the major changes the Motor Carrier Act made was to reduce the requirements for a motor carrier to enter a market. In the past, a carrier had to prove there was a need for additional service in the desired area.

With deregulation, a carrier needs only to show the desire and ability to provide service to the market in question. A second major change was that restrictions were removed on operating authority. Previously a carrier might be authorized to carry steel from Chicago to St. Louis but only by way of Indianapolis and not be authorized to carry any commodities back to Chicago. Deregulation removed these restrictions. A third change was the establishment of rate change zones. Previously, a carrier had to obtain ICC approval before changing a rate, either up or down. Deregulation provided for carriers to raise or lower their rates within established zones without ICC approval. A fourth change was the provision for freight brokers. Brokers arrange transportation between a shipper and carrier for a fee. Prior to deregulation only 10 freight broker licenses had been issued in 43 years. Ten years after deregulation that number was over 5,000.[5] A fifth change was that carriers could transport regulated and exempt cargo in the same trailer. Previously, a carrier could not transport exempt cargo, such as agricultural products, with other regulated cargo.

The effects of deregulation have, by and large, been positive. Deregulation has increased competition and reduced both less-than-truckload (LTL) and truckload (TL) rates. There has been a major shakeout in carriers, with 10 of the top 20 LTL carriers in 1978 having declared bankruptcy by 1988. Also, private carriers can now apply to become contract or common carriers and solicit business to reduce empty backhauls. An additional benefit of improved efficiency is energy conservation through reduced fuel consumption.

Staggers Rail Act of 1980
The primary benefit of the Staggers Rail Act has been the deregulation of rates. Fundamentally, rates have been deregulated where there is open competition. Where market dominance occurs, minimum and maximum rates were established. As in the Motor Carrier Act, a zone of rate freedom was established. Additionally, rail carriers' rate increases are now tied to the inflation rate. Probably the most important provision was the legalization of long-term contracts between railroads and large-volume shippers. Prior to deregulation, the railroads were generally tied to using the established rates with little flexibility. The contract must be filed with the ICC, but the actual rates may remain confidential. Another major change was

---

[5]Lambert and Stock, p. 182.

that railroads were allowed to abandon service of many nonprofitable routes and roadbeds. Prior to deregulation, they were required to maintain service on many routes by the ICC and could abandon service only after obtaining approval.

Deregulation has been a positive experience for the rail industry as a whole. Profitability is up while inflation-adjusted rates are down. The rail industry has become more creative in the services it offers to shippers because of its ability to enter into long-term contracts. For example, Union Pacific was able to negotiate a backhaul contract for fertilizer to make use of grain cars that were delivering to Gulf ports like New Orleans. Before deregulation, the contract would not have been possible because of the open nature of the rate-setting process.[6] Prior to deregulation, not only would other rail lines have the ability to participate in the rate-setting decision, but the water carriers could also have participated and even potentially blocked the service since it could take business away from them.

Airline Deregulation Acts of 1977 and 1978

The 1977 act focused primarily on air cargo while the 1978 act was more oriented to passenger traffic. The primary benefit of airline deregulation was that it opened operating authority. That is, any carrier could become an all-cargo carrier. Additionally, by 1982 all carriers, both passenger and cargo, could enter any market they desired. Freight rates were also deregulated and did not have to be filed.

Deregulation has not been favorable to the airline industry. The increased competition has caused a major revision in air cargo providers. In 1978, 84 percent of air freight was handled by passenger or combination airlines and 16 percent by all-cargo carriers. By 1989 the numbers were reversed.[7] This decrease in air freight revenues for passenger carriers has no doubt hurt their profitability.

Shipping Act of 1984

Rates in maritime shipping have traditionally been formed by shipper conferences, which are groups of shippers who establish rates, decide which ports to serve, pool cargo, and share the revenues for international

---

[6]Donald F. Wood and James C. Johnson, *Contemporary Transportation,* 4th ed. (New York: Macmillan Publishing Company, 1993), p. 130.

[7]Lambert and Stock, p. 203.

deep sea shipping. The main thrust of the Shipping Act was to reinforce the use of conferences by providing greater antitrust immunity. On the rate side, the Act reduced the time for implementation of new rates to 45 days and allows individual carriers to deviate from the conference rate with 10 days notice. Additionally, carriers could use service contracts similar to rail; like rail contracts they had to be filed with the FMC. Also, allowing carriers to establish point-to-point intermodal rates has increased the competitiveness of the maritime industry and provided the ability to offer complete service to shippers.

Freight Rates and Costs

Freight rates are established on the basis of a variety of factors. The first factor is the class of an item. An item's class is based on its density, or pounds per cubic foot (the greater the density, the lower the rate per pound); its stowability (excessive weight or length increases the charges); its ease of handling (any special care or additional handling increases the rate); liability to damage and theft (the greater the value per pound, the greater the risk of theft and the liability for damage); and its value (the higher the value of an item, the greater transportation cost it can afford). The second factor is the distance the item is to be moved. The greater the distance, the lower the cost per mile, as many of the fixed costs of operating the carrier are spread over a greater number of miles. A third factor is the weight of the shipment. Normally rates are based on one of three quantities:

1. Truckload (TL), carload (CL), or container load rates, which are the lowest and apply only to the minimum weight that effectively uses the entire trailer, railcar, or container. For example, a TL rate may be based on 36,000 pounds.
2. Less-than-truckload (LTL) or less-than-carload (LCL) rates are for weights less than the TL or CL minimums.
3. Any quantity (AQ) rate, which gives no discount for greater volumes.

A fourth consideration is the cost of service, which may include costs of terminal operations and handling as well as any applicable taxes and fees.

Line-haul Rates
Line-haul rates are the rates associated with moving product between two or more points. They are divided into four types: class, exception, commodity,

and miscellaneous rates. Class rates are the basic rate for moving a commodity between two points based on the product. For example, to move 40,000 pounds of cellulose film between Belvidere, New Jersey, and New York City, the class rate is $1.22 per hundred pounds (cwt). Exception rates are special rates, lower than class rates, to provide a special rate for a specific area, origin, destination, or commodity when competition or volume justify the lower rate. For the same example, an exception rate exists of $0.85 per cwt. Commodity rates are for large quantities of a product that are shipped between two locations on a regular basis. Continuing the example, the commodity rate is $0.54 per cwt. Miscellaneous rates are rates that apply in special circumstances, such as contract rates. A common freight classification is FAK (freight-all-kinds), which establishes a rate based on cost of service, not on product class.

Other Service Charges
Service charges can be divided into two groups, terminal services and line-haul services. Terminal services, which may be additional to the line-haul rate, include pickup and delivery between the shipper and the carrier's terminal; loading or unloading of the trailer, container, or railcar; and demurrage (rail) or detention (motor carrier) charges, which are charges for keeping a railcar or trailer beyond the specified time allowed for unloading.

Line-haul service charges are for services provided while the shipment is being moved between locations. One charge is for stopping in transit. This includes either picking up additional items or splitting deliveries of a load between two or more locations. Another charge is for reconsignment and diversion, that is, changing the ownership of the shipment or its delivery point while the shipment is in transit. Pooling charges are for either consolidating incoming shipments into a truckload or carload quantity for delivery to one location or for delivery of several LTL or LCL shipments shipped as a carload or truckload shipment to several destinations. Transit privilege charges allow a shipment to be stopped in transit, work to be performed on it, and then the delivery to be completed. The last group of line-haul services is for protective services such as refrigeration, heating, ventilation, or security.

Documentation

The primary transportation document is the bill of lading. The bill of lading "originates the shipment, provides all the information for the carrier to accomplish the move, stipulates the transportation contract terms, acts as a receipt for the goods tendered to the carrier, and, in some cases, shows certificate of title to the goods."[8] A straight bill of lading is nonnegotiable as opposed to an order bill of lading, which is a negotiable instrument that shows title of the goods specified. Order bills allow the shipper to withhold delivery until payment is received; if the customer is unable to pay, the shipper could sell the goods to another party. Export bills of lading permit the domestic use of export rates for the goods that are being exported. The export rates may be lower than the normal domestic rate for the domestic line-haul portion. The transportation contract terms include issues such as carrier liability for loss or delay, charges for storage on freight not accepted by customer, and recourse for additional freight charges. A bill of lading signed by the receiving party usually functions as a delivery receipt.

The second most important transportation document is the freight bill, which is the carrier's bill for the transportation services performed. A bill may be prepaid, which means that the freight charges are presented before the service is performed. A collect bill means that the consignee must pay the freight charges at the time of delivery. Railroads are permitted to extend credit up to five days, while motor carriers can extend credit up to seven days. No discount is permitted for early payment of freight charges.

Documents used in international shipments in addition to the bill of lading include import/export license, import/export declaration, certificate of origin, invoice, statement of charges, packing list, inspection or analysis certificate, and insurance certificate. Any error or omission in any of these documents can result in significant delays in movement of the goods.

Freight Claims

Freight claims take two basic forms: losses and overcharges. Losses include losses due to the destruction or disappearance of an item, damage to the item, and delay in the item's delivery. Carriers are responsible for losses or damage sustained in transit and for unreasonable delay. Carriers are not liable for losses due to acts of God unless those events are foreseeable. For instance, a truckload of goods moving between Laramie, Wyoming, and Boise, Idaho, is delayed due to a snowstorm in late July.

---

[8]John J. Coyle and Edward J. Bardi, *The Management of Business Logistics,* 3rd ed. (St. Paul, Minn.: West Publishing Company, 1984), p. 326.

This act was probably not foreseeable, but if the shipment was made in December it would be expected. Claims for losses must be submitted within nine months of delivery. The carrier then has 30 days to acknowledge receipt of the claim and must notify the claimant of its intention to pay or reject the claim within 120 days. The onus of proof of loss is on the claimant. Thus, upon receipt of damaged goods, it is imperative to begin collecting data on the additional costs incurred because of the loss or delay. Any goods that are visibly damaged on receipt should be noted on the receiving documents. A useful tool to have is an instant camera on the receiving dock to take pictures of damaged goods as they are received. As the goods are unpacked, any damage that was hidden from initial inspection should be noted. With concealed damage, the difficulty is proving where the damage occurred, before or after receipt or even before shipment. Labels or other measurement devices that indicate shocks received or exposure to elements can be useful indicators of potential damage even though the shipping container appears undamaged.

Given the complexity of the rate determination system, overcharges are common. Since there are requirements for prompt payment, within five to seven days, there is normally not enough time to verify that the transportation charges are correct. Thus the shipping or receiving organization must pay the charges and file a claim if overcharges are discovered. Overcharge claims may be filed up to three years after delivery. Many firms use freight auditors to review shipping charges. Typically the auditors receive a percentage of all overcharges they are able to recover. Overcharges can occur when a shipper does not identify the product in the most advantageous class, is not aware of exception or commodity rates, or does not ship an item by the most advantageous weight category. For example, 4,600 pounds of an item at $2.52 per hundred weight would cost $115.92 ($2.52 x 46). But the same shipment could be shipped at $1.93 per hundred weight, the 5,000 pounds rate, for $96.50 ($1.93 x 50). Thus a 17 percent savings could be made by simply reclassifying the shipment's weight.

Carrier Sourcing

Selecting a carrier or carriers for inbound transportation is fundamentally the same process as selecting any other supplier. The first step is to determine the firm's current inbound transportation costs, volumes, and areas where suppliers are located. Also, any special delivery requirements, such as just-in-time or freight consolidation requirements, need to be identified.

The second step is to identify potential transportation providers. Issues to consider in selecting potential transportation providers include:

Does the potential carrier specialize or offer programs on inbound logistics?

How flexible is the carrier when delivery requirements change?

Can the carrier provide help in managing inbound freight?

What is the carrier's damage claim performance, claims process, and response time?

Does the carrier focus on high-quality service?

Third, as proposals are submitted they need to be reviewed for anticipated savings, potential for internal productivity savings, and discounts. Also, will the plan improve control of inbound transportation and reduce overcharges?[9]

Transportation Control

A key service of any transportation provider is its ability to track and potentially expedite any shipment. To facilitate the tracing of any shipment the shipper should be able to provide the bill of lading number, the origin of the shipment, date of origin, destination, a description of the goods, the carrier, and if possible the car or trailer number. The technology of today has improved the ability of carriers to trace shipments. Automatic scanning of rail car numbers by trackside sensors and satellite tracking systems for trucks have made it possible to have up-to-the-minute information on the location of goods anywhere in North America.

Another aspect of transportation control is auditing of freight bills. Whether this function is done internally or by a freight auditing firm, given the legal requirements for quick payment, after the fact follow-up is critical to avoid overcharges and undercharges.

Freight Contracting

One of the primary benefits of deregulation in transportation has been the increased ability to negotiate contracts and rates with carriers for specific

---

[9]James Watson, "Criteria for Selecting an Inbound Freight Carrier," *Inbound Traffic Guide*, January 1983, pp. 86–87.

services or service packages. For example, 80 percent of all rail traffic now is covered by a contract. The key things to remember in contracting with carriers are that the proposed rate must not be below the carrier's costs, the rate the carrier offers must be available to all shippers that meet the same conditions, and the rate cannot act to reduce competition.

Both rates and services can be negotiated with a potential carrier. An example of a rate-related issue might be development of a description and rate for rejected goods. Since rejected goods have a lower value, they would fall in a lower class, thereby qualifying for a lower rate. Another example might occur if a shipper were willing to release the carrier from full value liability of the goods, thus reducing the carrier's liability and thereby qualifying for a lower rate. A third example might be to include or eliminate the costs of loading and unloading the carrier's equipment. A final example is to negotiate a mileage rate regardless of the goods.

A service that could be negotiated is the number of stops in transit allowed. Also, the scheduling of pickup and delivery could be negotiated to provide better service. For example, a sporting goods wholesaler has a carrier pick up its trailer every day during the late afternoon. The carrier brings an empty trailer for the next day's shipments and picks up the full trailer. The carrier avoids multiple pickups from one location and minimizes its turnaround time. The shipper is assured of regular service. Another service that could be negotiated is to allow the carrier the option of deferred delivery, within specified ranges, so it can make better use of its equipment, thus reducing its costs. Finally, maximum transit times could be negotiated to ensure delivery within specified time frames.

Although deregulation allows negotiated rates, carriers are still required to file negotiated rates with the ICC each and every time the rates change. As competition increased after deregulation, many carriers began offering discounts off the published tariffs but neglected to file the new rates with the ICC. As many of these carriers began to go bankrupt, trustees of the bankrupt carriers began auditing old freight bills and discovered the discrepancies between regular published rates and unfiled discounts. Thus, to recover as much money as they could for the creditors, trustees began to bill shippers for the difference between the rate paid and the published tariff. The shippers fought the claims, and the ICC upheld the shippers' arguments through the Negotiated Rates Policy. The Federal Circuit Courts also upheld the ICC position, but in June 1990 the Supreme Court ruled that the ICC's Negotiated Rates Policy was invalid and that only legally filed tariffs could be used in establishing transportation charges.

In 1993, Congress passed the Negotiated Rates Act to address the problem of undercharges. According to the act, the filed rate doctrine is still in force and the ICC is instructed to enforce tariffs strictly in the future; motor carrier contracts must be in writing, identify the parties involved, include the rates, cover a series of shipments, and provide for dedicated equipment or meet a distinct need; and discounts by common and contract carriers to anyone other than the firm paying the bill are illegal.[10] The act provides for the option for settlement of an undercharge claim for 20 percent of the claim for LTL shipments and 15 percent for TL shipments. Additionally, shippers may fight the claim using a variety of defenses, including the unreasonable practice defense that was thrown out by the Supreme Court in its earlier decision. Another major change is that the statute of limitations for undercharge claims is reduced from three years to 18 months.

Preventive actions can be taken to reduce the risk of undercharge claims in the future. First, demand a letter from the ICC verifying that the rates have been filed. Second, do not use a negotiated rate until verification has been received from the ICC, including the effective date of the tariffs. Remember, an overcharge claim can be filed if the tariff becomes effective and the firm pays the higher rate. Finally, if the firm does receive an undercharge claim, do not assume it is valid. Verify that the shipment was actually made; that the firm was responsible for the charges, i.e., that the goods were not shipped collect or that the shipper had invoked the "no recourse" clause on a prepaid shipment; that the statute of limitations has not expired; that an applicable tariff was in force at the time of the shipment; that the proper tariff is being applied, i.e., an exception or commodity tariff may have been in force; that the freight is properly described; and that the rate was properly selected and calculated.[11]

INCOMING PACKAGING REQUIREMENTS

The packaging used for incoming materials is important to the purchaser for several reasons. First, the packaging will control the risk of damage to

---

[10]Thomas A. Foster, "Two Cheers for the Negotiated Rates Act," *Distribution,* December 1993, p. 4.

[11]Stanley Hoffman, "Basic Defenses to Beat Undercharge Claims," *Distribution,* September 1990, pp. 89–90.

incoming material. Second, appropriate packaging can facilitate material handling and control. Third, the purchasing department may have the responsibility to dispose of the used packaging material, so any actions that can either reduce the amount of packaging material or make it easier to dispose of will have value to the firm. With this in mind, let us look at the functions of packaging, package design considerations, recycling considerations, and hazardous materials requirements.

Functions of Packaging

The six functions of packaging that apply to both industrial packaging and consumer packaging are: containment, protection, apportionment, unitization, convenience, and communication.

The first function is the containment of the product, allowing it to be moved from one location to another in an economical fashion. Packaging provides a structure that allows materials to be moved in large quantities.

Protection is multifaceted. The first element of protection is to protect the item or items from damage caused by the shipping process. Items are subject to a variety of shocks and vibrations during shipment and without proper protection could be damaged easily. A second element is to protect the item or items from damage due to the environment. Products may be damaged by exposure to wind, rain, snow, temperature extremes, or sunlight. A third element is to protect the environment from the material in the package. An example is the packaging around chemicals or nuclear waste. A fourth element of protection, more commonly found in the retail sector, is protection from theft. Packages that are difficult to open or are bulky discourage theft.

The apportionment function of packaging puts the product into usable quantities. Green beans could be shipped in 10-pound units that would reduce the packaging requirements but very few of us can make use of 10 pounds of green beans at one time. Apportionment by packaging in the manufacturing process often involves designing containers for shipping that hold a standard quantity, such as a day's or an hour's worth of production. This way, firms can reduce their inventory and improve the accuracy of the inventory records.

The unitization function of packaging allows the creation of large shipping units from individual product packages, which can be handled more efficiently for transportation. An example is putting cans into a cardboard box, stacking the boxes on a pallet, and then shrink-wrapping the pallet. The cardboard boxes allow the product to be stacked easily while the shrink-wrapping reduces the movement of the boxes on the pallet, reducing the risk of damage.

The convenience function deals with the ease of use of the packaged product. We have all dealt with packaging that was hard to open. The easier the package is to open, the greater the opportunity to reuse the packaging, but this also increases the risk of theft or product tampering. An example of a packaging trade-off is the design of one-gallon antifreeze containers. The container would be easier to ship if it was rectangular, but its ease of use in pouring would be seriously diminished.

The final function of packaging is to provide information about the contents of the package. Once an item is packaged and hidden from view, the packaging must provide information about the contents. A package label should perform a variety of functions. First, it should identify the contents by part number, product description, and quantity. Additionally, labels on consumer packaging may have to meet regulatory requirements such as those required by the Federal Drug Administration. A label may also indicate damage or the potential for damage to the contents. Special labels can be attached to a shipping container to indicate that the package has been subjected to shocks above a particular force, tilted, or exposed to the elements such as sunlight and moisture. Third, the package should give any special storage or handling instructions such as "This end up" or "Keep in cool location."

Package Design

What constitutes a good package design? The answer to this question depends on a variety of factors. One consideration is the ability to hold industry standard quantities of an item. The definition of standard quantity depends on the application. In chemicals, for instance, standard quantities might be gallons, liters, barrels, or 50-pound bags, while for copy paper the standard quantity might be reams. A second consideration is the cost of the packaging. Packaging normally does not add value to a product, only cost to both the producer and the user. Any packaging that can be reduced, eliminated, or recycled is preferable. A third consideration is the protection level the package needs to provide. The packaging should be designed to withstand the normal shocks and vibrations that the product will receive during the shipping and storage process. A fourth consideration is the handling ability of the package. Square or rectangular packages are easier to stack and move than odd-shaped packages. However, square or rectangular packages may not be the easiest to use or pour. They may not be as attractive to the customer. The tradeoff is the extra cost for packaging unused space both in material used and cost to transport. A fifth consideration is the packageability of the product itself.

Recycling Considerations

It is becoming more important for purchasers to consider the materials used in packaging. How will a product's packaging materials be disposed of or reused? Hewlett Packard uses foam packaging material as a tray to move product through assembly and then uses the tray to protect the product in shipping. Many organizations design their boxes that move material from distribution centers to retail outlets to be broken down easily and returned to the distribution center for reuse. Chemical distributors have long encouraged the reuse of barrels. The shrink-wrap used for unitizing pallet loads can be recycled into plastic resin. If packaging cannot be reused, efforts should be made to reduce the packaging material or use recyclable materials.

Hazardous Materials

A hazardous material is any substance or material that has been determined by the Secretary of Transportation to be capable of posing an unreasonable risk to health, safety, and property when transported in commerce. The list of hazardous materials includes over 33,000 commodities. The Hazardous Materials Transportation Uniform Safety Act of 1990 covers the transportation of hazardous materials. Previously, packaging requirements for hazardous materials were specified in detail, including the construction of the packaging material. Recently, hazardous material package qualifications were modified to be based on performance, not construction. A hazardous material package needs to withstand shock such as dropping, moisture, crushing when stacked, and vibration and maintain structural integrity even when damaged. Any firm shipping hazardous material is responsible for the effects of that shipment if an accident occurs. Thus purchasing must ensure that the packaging is certified.

RECEIVING

Receiving is responsible for verifying that the goods received are the goods the firm ordered. The first step in the receiving process is to receive the goods from the carrier, which may include unloading the carrier's vehicle. The consignee has the responsibility to count the boxes, pallets, etc. of the shipment to verify that the number of packages received matches the bill of lading.

Second, the consignee inspects the packages for visible freight damage. If shipping damage is found, the damage should be noted on the bill of lading and the carrier must sign the bill of lading acknowledging the damage. The consignee should not sign the bill of lading acknowledging receipt until the damage is acknowledged. If the entire shipment is damaged, the consignee may reject delivery of the entire shipment but should not do so without appropriate instructions from purchasing or the user.

After receipt of the shipment, the packing list should be compared both with the purchase order and against the goods actually received. Any discrepancies should be noted and communicated to purchasing. Verification is made of both the specific items and the quantities received. While unpacking the goods, the receiver is also inspecting for any obvious damage that was hidden by the packaging.

The receiver completes all the necessary paperwork, or computer data entry, including notification to purchasing of any shortages, back orders, or open items. Normally notification of receipt goes to the requisitioner, purchasing, accounts payable, and quality assurance.

The final step in the receiving process is the disposition of the material. In a dock-to-stock system this entails delivery of the goods to the using point. In a traditional system, movement may be to incoming quality inspection or directly into a warehouse for storage.

The proper identification of materials is a continual challenge. Receiving is where the firm's part numbers should be applied to the material as it is received. There are a number of ways to accomplish this task, including bar coding, discussed in Chapter 2. Before an item leaves receiving it should be identified by part number and its disposition recorded.

Receiving services is more difficult because they do not usually come through the normal receiving operation. The user becomes responsible for indicating when the services were received and that they were of acceptable quality. The best control of services is achieved by indicating on the purchase order the services to be performed and the acceptance criteria. A formal acknowledgment of receipt should be sent to accounts payable so that they may pay upon receipt of an invoice.

WAREHOUSE AND STORES MANAGEMENT

The other component of inbound logistics is the management of goods once they are received and before they are used by the requisitioner. There are two primary storage mediums, warehouse and stores. On the inbound side, the purpose of a warehouse is to hold material that is received in larger quantities than the requisitioner requires immediately and to hold material that is received well in advance of the requirement. On the outbound side, a warehouse serves to accumulate products for shipment, hold inventory created for uncertainty of demand or to take advantage of economies of scale, and to shorten transportation distances by moving the product closer to the customer.

The layout of a warehouse depends on a number of factors, such as the size of the material to be stored, the disbursement quantities, and frequency of disbursements. The larger and heavier the items being stored, the greater the need for wide aisles to allow the use of large lift trucks to access the material. The disbursement quantities help to determine how much material to store at each location. For example, material that is received by the case but disbursed one unit at a time will probably be stored in units on a shelf with the excess at a second location. Frequency affects layout, as it is generally desirable to locate high-volume items at the ends of an aisle and as low as possible. Basically, the higher that one goes in the storage racks and the farther away from a main aisle, the lower should be the frequency of access. Another organizational rationale is to group parts that have a high probability of being used together. The objective of good warehouse design is to minimize the handling of material that adds no value to the customer. Ideally, many items should be stored as close to the user as possible, eliminating intermediate handling between the warehouse and the user.

A common function of a warehouse is to assemble materials for an order. The order may be for internal use or for the firm's customer. There are several options for order picking organization. The traditional approach is to assign one picker to an order or part of an order and have that individual pick the parts for the order no matter what the location in the warehouse. A second approach is to assign pickers to a specified area in the warehouse to pick all the parts stored in that area. A third approach is to dedicate workers to specific products. A fourth approach is to assign teams to specific customers to assemble all the orders for those customers.

The stores area is a special warehouse within the firm where parts are disbursed in small quantities but are bought in larger quantities to reduce acquisition costs. A closed stores system is one where the materials are stored in a closed area with limited access. The purpose is to restrict access and thereby reduce the risk of loss and improve inventory accuracy. Parts with high value or that require careful storage or handling are prime candidates for closed stores. In an open stores system, the material is stored either close to the user or in a central area, but anyone has access to the material. Parts with high usage and/or low value are prime candidates for storage in an open system. For example, many firms keep operating supplies in an open system.

A prime difference between an open and a closed stores system is in the record keeping. By controlling the disbursement of materials with a closed stores system, the focus is on keeping high inventory accuracy, usually through the use of a perpetual inventory system. Open systems monitor needs by simple control systems such as periodic review or simple reorder systems such as the two-bin system discussed in Chapter 3. Material costs are calculated by estimating usage based upon output and the changes in inventory levels, rather than on actual usage as indicated by the documentation in a closed system.

PURCHASING RESPONSIBILITIES

What does all this discussion of inbound logistics issues have to do with purchasing? In a 1988 Center for Advanced Purchasing Studies report, one of the areas in which purchasing had assumed an increasing role was the area of traffic and transportation.[12] This, coupled with the increased interest in just-in-time delivery, has made transportation a very important issue in the supply process.

One of the opportunities open to purchasing is the consolidation of inbound materials. For example, instead of using inbound LTL shipments from local suppliers, Xerox picks up 100 stock keeping units (SKUs) from 25 suppliers within a 50-mile radius. Also, there is a daily pickup from one

[12]Harold E. Fearon, *Purchasing Organizational Relationships* (Tempe, Ariz.: Center for Advanced Purchasing Studies, 1988), p. 16.

main supplier and several smaller suppliers in Chicago, 600 miles away, through an independent freight consolidator. Similarly, Harley Davidson operates a daily shuttle to pick up mixed load from several suppliers within 200 miles of its York, Pennsylvania, plant. Its suppliers more than 200 miles away ship to consolidation points in Aurora, Illinois, or Cleveland, Ohio. There, shipments from approximately 60 suppliers are loaded onto two trucks for transfer to York. Both companies have experienced a reduction in their inbound freight costs through the use of truckload quantities as well as a reduction in inventories by the use of smaller shipping quantities for each item.

Purchasing also may alter its ordering patterns to take advantage of opportunities to reduce inbound freight costs. For example, rather than ordering a larger amount from a supplier to obtain the benefits of truckload or carload transportation rates, purchasing could ascertain if any other items provided by that supplier or another supplier in the same general area could be ordered, allowing the buyer to still take advantage of truckload or carload rates, while at the same time keeping inventory levels down.

As firms begin to reduce their supply bases, the same potential exists for reducing the number of carriers. Increased opportunities to contract with carriers, provided by deregulation, coupled with a reduction in the organization's supply base, provide many opportunities to reduce transportation costs. For example, a chemical distributor had five warehouses within a circle with a radius of about 100 miles. Regularly, interwarehouse transfers were made between the five warehouses, yet each warehouse used its own local common carrier whenever it needed to transfer material from one location to another. A single carrier could have been selected to provide the service throughout the region on a contract basis, giving scheduled service and lower costs based on the total volume of business. By developing preferred relationships with carriers, purchasing has the opportunity to reduce incoming freight costs by negotiating special commodity rates or discount rates, provide better service, and take advantage of private carriers.

The increasing trends of order consolidation and JIT delivery are creating challenges to receiving as well. The presence of multiple orders in one shipment increases the problems of accurate identification of materials for receiving. Also, the potential increased frequency of delivery and even direct delivery to the user by the supplier will increase control problems.

CHAPTER SUMMARY

This chapter has examined the issues involved in inbound logistics, including packaging, transportation, receiving, and warehouse management. Key points are:

- The major modes of transportation include water, motor carrier, air, rail, pipeline, intermodal combinations, and nonshippers.
- Carrier types are common, contract, exempt, and private.
- Rail, motor carrier, air, and water transportation have all undergone major deregulation since 1977, resulting in increased competition and greater freedom to negotiate contracts for transportation.
- Freight rates are based on the class of an item, distance to be moved, weight of the shipment, cost of service, and value of the service.
- Line-haul rates cover the movement of product between two or more points and consist of four types—class, exception, commodity, and miscellaneous.
- Service rates are for additional terminal or line-haul services such as demurrage or detention, stopping in transit, or pooling charges.
- Transportation documentation includes the bill of lading, freight bill, and manifest.
- Freight claims can be for losses due to damage, loss, or delay of an item and for overcharges.
- Deregulation has increased the firm's ability to negotiate contracts with carriers for rates and services. An important issue with negotiated rates is that they must be filed with the appropriate agency. Anyone negotiating such discounts should insist on proof of filing to prevent undercharge claims at a later date.
- Packaging can be a major cost component of incoming material. More attention to incoming packaging can reduce the cost of material as well as the cost of disposing of the packaging material.
- Recycling of packaging material is of rising concern to purchasing and a possible way to reduce packaging costs.
- Hazardous material packaging and shipping needs to be closely monitored to reduce the firm's liability.

- Purchasing needs to pay more attention to the consolidation of inbound freight by consolidating shipments from multiple suppliers or by ordering several items from the same supplier.
- A reduction in the number of inbound carriers can mean better service and lower rates through contracting for carrier services for larger volumes.

REFERENCES

Bowersox, Donald J., David J. Closs, and Omar K. Helferich. *Logistical Management,* 3rd ed. New York: Macmillan Publishing Company, 1986.

Coyle, John J., and Edward J. Bardi. *The Management of Business Logistics,* 3rd ed. St. Paul, Minn.: West Publishing Company, 1984.

Dobler, Don W., David N. Burt, and Lee Lamar, Jr. *Purchasing and Materials Management,* 5th ed. New York: McGraw-Hill Publishing Company, 1990.

Glaskowsky, Jr., Nicholas A., Donald R. Hudson, and Robert M. Ivie. *Business Logistics,* 3rd ed. Fort Worth, Tex.: The Dryden Press, 1992.

Johnson, James C., and Donald F. Wood. *Contemporary Logistics,* 5th ed. New York: Macmillan Publishing Company, 1993.

Lambert, Douglas M., and James R. Stock. *Strategic Logistics Management,* 3rd ed. Homewood, Ill.: Richard D. Irwin, Inc., 1993.

Wood, Donald F., and James C. Johnson. *Contemporary Transportation,* 4th ed. New York: Macmillan Publishing Company, 1993.

SECTION 4

ANCILLARY SUPPLY FUNCTIONS

CHAPTER 6

ANCILLARY SUPPLY FUNCTIONS

INTRODUCTION

Diversified Technology, a small manufacturing firm, applied value analysis to the design and manufacture of a portable device for resetting fire alarm control panels during system testing. The original design had 24 hand-soldered hook-up wires, which were replaced with a circuit board and two hook-up wires resulting in a 38 percent cost reduction. Overall, the number of parts was reduced from 85 to 51, scrap and rework were virtually eliminated, and overall manufacturing costs were reduced by 38 percent.[1]

The example above illustrates the use of many of the topics discussed in this chapter. Diversified Technology used the concepts of value analysis and standardization to reduce the product's cost of manufacture, which included the materials' costs. Chapter 6 deals with a variety of topics centered around reducing inventory, material, and operating costs through standardization and simplification, value analysis/engineering, cost reduction programs, and surplus and disposal activities. The role and responsibilities of purchasing in these activities will be examined.

STANDARDIZATION PROGRAMS

Standardization is the process of defining a set of materials, parts, and components to be used by the firm. A standard may indicate either a commonality of parts, such as the same switch across a variety of electric drill sizes, or a minimum level of performance, such as an ASTM standard. Standardization differs from simplification in that simplification is elimi-

---

[1]Ernest Raia, "Value Analysis 1993," *Purchasing,* June 3, 1993, pp. 56–59.

nating unnecessary functions, features, or tasks while standardization is reducing the number of different parts performing the same or similar functions.

Standards can be government specified, industry based, or company specified. Government standards deal with regulations and codes such as hazardous materials transportation and packaging, content labeling on foods, or product standards. Industry based standards are commonly agreed upon specifications for a wide variety of products such as fasteners, wire gages, bar codes, and wood grades. Company specified standards are specifications for items, procedures, or services that the firm may produce, perform, or purchase. Establishing company standards is a management decision-making process that identifies a requirement and then selects a product to fill that requirement wherever and whenever it occurs. The organization may use an industry standard item or a custom product if no industry standard product meets the requirements.

Many industry standards are established through national and international standards organizations such as the American National Standards Institute (ANSI), American Society for Testing and Materials (ASTM), American Society of Mechanical Engineers (ASME), Society of Automotive Engineers (SAE), Underwriters' Laboratories (UL), and International Standards Organization (ISO). These organizations work to develop national and international consensus standards by helping the participants to reach agreement on the need for a standard and priorities of the standard. There are approximately 12,000 ANSI-approved standards, including such areas as computer languages, electronic data interchange protocols and forms, and quality certification requirements.

Benefits of Standardization

There are a variety of benefits related to effective standardization within a company. The most common benefits deal with inventory. Reducing the number of different items used will reduce the number of items to be stored, lowering space requirements, and should reduce the value of the inventory. For example, if two items, each with the same average demand and standard deviation per period, were standardized into one item, the safety stock requirements would decline about 40 percent for the same level of service. Standardization also improves inventory performance by increasing the fill rate for items. Since there are fewer items to stock, the chances of the item not being available are reduced.

Another set of benefits from standardization are created by the increases in volume. Normally higher volumes lead to lower unit prices. Custom items cost more than standard items.

> A survey of representative manufacturers of industrial products revealed the following significant cost comparisons: 23 percent of the manufacturers estimated that special items cost from 10 to 15 percent more to produce than comparable standard items; 47 percent estimated the additional cost at from 25 to 50 percent; 17 percent estimated that the extra cost ran even higher than 50 percent. Only 12 percent estimated that no substantial extra cost was involved.[2]

Also, standardization can lead to the more effective use of systems contracts as the needs are more clearly defined.

Standardization decreases control costs. Fewer items means less time spent counting inventory and a less complicated system to control inventory. Also, maintenance can improve their proficiency when equipment and repair parts are standardized.

Standardization can help decrease new product introduction time as the design engineers are able to use common components with a proven track record of reliability and availability. This also reduces purchasing's need to find a new source for new items. By standardizing its inventory of overhead items used in satellites, Hughes Aircraft was not only able to save approximately $150,000 a year, they were also able to reduce delays in satellite delivery caused by the lack of overhead parts.[3]

The Standardization Process

The process to develop a standardization program follows the steps common for implementing any new program. The first step is to identify potential areas for standardization. Common areas to consider for standardization include: production materials, parts, tools, and equipment; construction materials and building supplies; packaging materials; material-handling equipment; production equipment; maintenance materials, such as lubricants; and office equipment, supplies, and forms.

---

[2]Stuart Heinritz, Paul V. Farrell, Larry Giunipero, and Michael Kolchin, *Purchasing: Principles and Applications,* 8th ed. (Englewood Cliffs, N.J.: Prentice Hall, 1991), p. 369.

[3]Christopher Allen and Patrick Allen, "Big Savings by Lower Echelons," *Production and Inventory Management Journal,* Second Quarter 1992, p. 71.

Second, a team or committee is formed with representation from the relevant areas. Relevant areas may include purchasing, maintenance, design engineering, plant engineering, marketing, production, and the customer. The purpose of wide representation is to avoid proposals that will not work because of failure to understand everyone's needs.

Third, data are collected on the current variety of items, the specifications for each item, the quantity requirements for each item, the cost of each item, the current stock level of each item, and the various applications of each item. The data are then analyzed looking for items with similar specifications as potential candidates to have one item meet several needs.

Next, a procedure is established for approving standards to be used in the future. It is not enough to standardize the current items; procedures must be put in place to avoid the proliferation of items in the future. For example, in product design, engineers are encouraged to use current parts and subassemblies rather than create new ones. One way to encourage the use of standard components is to create a catalog of authorized standard components. If new items are specified, they are studied to see if they can be used to replace an existing item or items.

A standardization program is usually implemented through attrition, where a nonstandard item is never replaced with another nonstandard item. If design changes are required, they must go through the normal processes, including customer involvement if appropriate. This may involve phasing out or surplusing items to be eliminated in conjunction with the parties involved.

Last, a process must be implemented to monitor and report the results regularly. Without regular follow-up, there will be an unchecked growth in nonstandard items over time.

COST REDUCTION AND AVOIDANCE PROGRAMS

Two of the most common measures of purchasing performance are cost reduction and cost avoidance savings. The Center for Advanced Purchasing Studies Purchasing Performance Benchmarks has indicated that 58 to 71 percent of the firms surveyed in several different industries set savings objectives. Normally savings targets seem to be in the 3 to 5 percent range.

There are several different approaches to obtaining cost reductions beyond the approach that General Motors recently took of informing suppliers they were expected to lower their prices by as much as 10 percent.

The goals of cost reduction programs are to identify and eliminate unnecessary costs and to obtain cost efficiencies without adversely affecting the quality and delivery performance of the items involved. Commonly used approaches include the use of organization-wide buying agreements, pool or cooperative purchasing, long-term agreements, and the contracting of total requirements. Each of these will be discussed in the following sections.

Organization-wide Buying Agreements

One approach to reducing the cost of purchased goods and services is to use organization-wide buying agreements. An organization-wide buying agreement is an agreement between a supplier and the buying organization to supply items throughout the buying organization, no matter the location. These can be administered in several ways, such as through centralized buying, by having one business unit or division take the responsibility of negotiating a contract with a supplier, or by using commodity councils.

Centralized Buying
Under centralized buying, the corporate purchasing function determines the needs of the various divisions and/or facilities, selects the supplier, and negotiates the terms of the agreement. This approach works well when there are common requirements across several divisions or facilities, when the requirements of any one division or facility are not large enough to obtain the best prices, or when there are supply shortages (to eliminate divisions bidding against each other for supply). For example, a large electronics firm decentralized all of its purchasing to the various divisions. The process worked fine until selected commodities became in short supply. To obtain material, division buyers found themselves in a bidding contest with other customers. Subsequently, management discovered that divisions had been bidding against other divisions of the company for supply from the same supplier. This led to the development of a centralized buying policy on selected commodities to prevent future occurrences of this situation.

Lead Division Buying
Lead division buying is similar to centralized buying except that instead of a centralized purchasing function arranging the contract, one division or business unit, usually the largest user of a commodity, negotiates the contract with the supplier. This approach is best when one business unit

or division uses the majority of a commodity. The firm is able to obtain lower prices due to the higher total volume and the supplier has to negotiate with only one division instead of several. Warn Industries, a manufacturer of winches and four-wheel drive hubs, reorganized the company into business units several years ago. One of the results was that the purchasing department was eliminated as each business unit took on the responsibility for its own procurement. To reduce confusion among the suppliers, various business units took the primary responsibility of communicating with specific suppliers. The lead business unit also had the responsibility of coordinating the internal users of the commodity to develop consistent specifications and requirements.

Commodity Councils
Commodity councils or teams include representatives from purchasing, users of the commodity, engineering, and quality. Each commodity council has the responsibility for selecting suppliers, negotiating contracts, and monitoring supplier performance, including quality and delivery performance. Commodity councils provide increased expertise for the procurement, increased communication between purchasing and the commodity users, increased control of the implementation of standardization programs, and improved communication with suppliers.[4] Commodities are selected by an analysis of usage, both quantity and dollar expenditures; technology; and relative importance to the firm's success.

Cooperative and Pooled Purchasing

Cooperative purchasing involves the establishment of a cooperative buying organization that negotiates pricing with suppliers based on the estimated total demand by the cooperative members. The cooperative then orders the material and delivers it to the members based upon their individual needs. Cooperatives are most commonly used by state and local governments, school districts, and hospitals. One source estimates that 50 to 70 percent of voluntary hospitals belong to one or more cooperatives.[5] The National

---

[4]Barbara Taylor-Cofield and Michael J. Kierdorf, "Commodity Management Teams at Texas Instruments," *Revolution in Purchasing and Materials Management,* 74th Annual International Purchasing Conference Proceedings (Tempe, Ariz.: National Association of Purchasing Management, 1989), p. 189.

[5]J. H. Holmgren and W. J. Wentz, *Material Management and Purchasing for the Health Care Facility* (Ann Arbor, Mich.: AUPHA Press, 1982), p. 276.

Association of Educational Buyers formed a cooperative, Educational and Institutional Cooperative Service, which provides its members with access to a number of furniture, supply, and service contracts.[6] Problems with cooperatives include lack of member commitment to using the cooperative, integrity of volume estimates with suppliers, and suppliers' fear of loss of profits.

Pooled purchasing occurs when one organization purchases the goods for several organizations at one time, and then upon receipt disburses the order to the participating organizations. For example, a buyer at one distribution center of a chemical distributor is about to order a truckload of sulfuric acid to keep the transportation costs as low as possible. Since a truckload will provide seven months of inventory based on current usage, the buyer contacts other distribution centers of the same company in the region to see if they are willing to share part of the order. If another center agrees, the order is placed and drop shipped, with part of the load going to each distribution center. Such activity can take place only within a company in the commercial sector but can take place more easily in the governmental and nonprofit sectors, as there are no antitrust restrictions for these sectors. The drawbacks of pooled purchasing include one organization having to pay the original bill and then collect from the other participants and the difficulty of coordinating orders between two or more organizations.

Long-term Agreements

Another way to reduce costs is to develop long-term agreements with suppliers to obtain better pricing and service over time rather than on a year-to-year basis. The supplier is able to provide lower prices knowing that any fixed costs associated with the contract can be amortized over a longer period.

Contracting Total Requirements

Total requirements contracting is committing to purchase from one supplier a certain item or items for the life of the product. By guaranteeing the supplier's participation throughout the life of the product, the supplier is able to make better decisions on investment requirements and even participate in product design knowing that it does not have to be concerned with losing the business on an annual or shorter term basis.

---

[6]Heinritz, Farrell, Giunipero, and Kolchin, p. 446.

VALUE ANALYSIS AND VALUE ENGINEERING

Value analysis was originally developed by Lawrence D. Miles of the General Electric purchasing organization and encouraged by Harry Erlicher, vice president of purchasing for General Electric at the time. The terms *value analysis* and *value engineering* are often used synonymously. However, the key difference is in the timing of the activity. Value engineering takes place during the product design phase while value analysis is usually associated with improvements after the product or service has been created. Design for manufacturability is a relatively recent approach that is in reality a variation of value engineering. The goal of both value analysis and value engineering is to attain the best product value to accomplish the required function at the least possible cost. Value of a product or service is defined as providing appropriate performance and cost. Value is increased when cost is reduced without reducing performance or performance is increased without increasing cost. Value analysis provides a process for evaluating the organization's cost reduction ideas, coordinating the affected parts of the organization, selling proposed improvements to management, implementing ideas, and documenting the cost reductions.

The value analysis function may be formal or informal in an organization. A firm could have a dedicated staff whose primary function is value analysis and engineering. Generally firms use an ad hoc approach, creating a value analysis team when it is deemed appropriate. The value analysis team should be cross functional with representatives from the areas involved, such as purchasing, engineering, materials, quality, production, customers, and suppliers. Even if a formal team is not established, purchasing has an ongoing responsibility to analyze the function and value of the items and services it is responsible for acquiring.

The Value Analysis Process

The value analysis process consists of six steps: identification, appraisal, solution generation, solution evaluation, implementation planning and execution, and project follow-up. Each of these steps is discussed below.

Identification
The identification step determines the functions of the item, the customer's requirements, the costs, the value of the functions, and the service and maintenance issues that are present. For each of these issues, the value

analysis team must identify the facts that are known about the item under analysis, the assumptions that are being made, and the information that is not known. The identification step provides the foundation for the value analysis process. The objective is to provide information from a variety of perspectives.

Appraisal

The purpose of the appraisal step is to investigate and prioritize the information created in the identification stage. The value analysis team first prioritizes the identified functions into primary and secondary functions by analyzing their relative importance to total performance. A cost/performance ratio can be identified for each function and used to evaluate the value of the function. For example, cost performance ratios might be dollars per pound or dollars per watt.

Solution Generation

This is where creativity enters the process. The objective is to identify alternative ways to do the job by determining what can be modified, simplified, combined, or eliminated in terms of functions, features, or processes. A number of techniques are discussed below that are useful in the generation of potential solutions.

Solution Evaluation

Once a set of potential solutions is generated, the next stage in the process is to evaluate the feasibility, appropriateness, and cost of each potential solution. The value analysis team must first determine if each solution is technically feasible. The team must also evaluate the suitability of a particular solution. For example, a knob used for turning on a burner on a stove could be replaced with a pair of pliers. Although the solution is technically feasible and may even have some safety benefits (for example, young children might have more difficulty using a pair of pliers), the average consumer would not find the solution acceptable. The cost of the various solutions must also be determined at this point. The goal of the value analysis process, to maintain or increase value while providing the same functionality at a reduced cost, must be remembered at this stage.

Implementation Planning and Execution

Once a preferred solution is identified, the team needs to develop a plan for making the required changes in the product and/or processes. This entails planning design changes, establishing completion and cost targets, and working with suppliers, if necessary, to implement the changes.

Project Follow-up
Probably the most important stage of the process is to verify that the project objectives were achieved. Has the item's total cost been reduced? Does the consumer perceive an increase or maintenance of value?

Value Analysis Techniques

Many techniques are available to help in the various stages of the value analysis process. These are discussed below.

Checklist
One approach especially useful in the solution generation stage is to use a checklist of questions such as the one in Table 6.1. By going through the checklist, the team ensures that the product is analyzed from a variety of perspectives. The checklist will also trigger the generation of a variety of ideas that may be missed with a technique such as brainstorming.

Functional cost approach
The functional cost approach involves determining the comparative costs of other approaches to providing the same function. As a company gains experience with a particular product or process, it can establish benchmark costs. As new products or processes are proposed, they can be evaluated by comparing what similar processes or products have cost in the past. Alternative ways to evaluate a product's value might be by weight or volume. A graph can be developed relating the weight of various items to their costs, and new products or improvements can be compared against the resulting curve. Any products that are not consistent are prime candidates for improvement.

Brainstorming
The purpose of brainstorming is to generate a large number of potential facts, ideas, or solutions in a relatively short time. This technique could be used in both the identification and solution generation stages. The technique involves the following steps: (1) review the topic, (2) review the ground rules for brainstorming, (3) allow time for thinking, (4) generate ideas, and (5) combine and eliminate similar ideas.

TABLE 6.1
Checklist for Value Analysis

Design

Can an item be eliminated?
If a nonstandard item, can a standard item be used in its place; if a standard
    item, is it the appropriate use of the item?
Does the item have a greater capacity than required?
Could a similar item in inventory be substituted?
Are tolerances too tight?
Are unnecessarily fine finishes being specified?
Is commercial quality specified?
Can the fasteners be standardized or even eliminated?
Can the item be handled easily?

Material

Can a different material be used?
Are standard materials being used?

Process

Is unnecessary machining being performed?
Is it cheaper to make or buy the item?
Can the item be produced using another process?
Is the process necessary?
Can scrap and waste be reduced?

Packaging

Can the packaging cost be reduced?
Can the packaging be reused?
Can a different packaging material be used?

Transportation

Can the weight be reduced?
Is the proper freight classification being used, both class and weight?
Is the load designed to minimize damage in transit?
Can the ease of handling and loading be improved?

Sourcing

Have suppliers been asked to suggest ways to reduce costs?
Could another supplier provide the item at a lower cost?
Could the cost be reduced through long-term contracts?

The first step is the most important, as it sets the stage by developing a clear problem statement. The statement is best stated as a "how," "why," or "what" question. For example, what are the functions performed by the knob on a stove burner's switch? Answers might include turning the burner on and off, indicating the level of heat, and providing aesthetic or decorative appeal.

The normal ground rules for brainstorming are relatively simple but often are difficult to enforce. First, all participants are encouraged to participate. No idea is too outlandish. Second, no discussion of ideas is allowed. Participants do not have to justify their ideas at this time. Third, no judgment is allowed; this will take place later. This includes comments as well as groans and facial expressions. Fourth, piggybacking on a previous idea is encouraged. Building upon each other's ideas is how truly creative solutions are generated. Last, the goal is to create as many ideas as possible. In problem solving, quantity breeds quality.

After everyone is clear about the process, give the participants some time to generate their own lists of ideas to share. The amount of time to allow will depend on the particular problem. Normally, two to five minutes is adequate.

As the ideas are generated, they should be recorded on a flip chart, overhead, or board so that everyone can see the complete list of ideas. One approach is to let the group put forth ideas randomly. This allows the group to freewheel and build upon each idea as it is recorded. An alternate approach is to go around the room, one person at a time, having each individual give one idea and then moving to the next person. Individuals have the right to pass on any round if they do not have a new idea to add at that time. The process continues until no one has any additional ideas. This structured approach ensures that everyone has an equal chance to participate and no one person dominates the session.

When the idea generation is ended, the group reviews the list. As each item is reviewed, it is compared against other ideas to see if it is essentially the same or should be combined with another idea. Also, the idea can be reviewed and discussed so that everyone understands what was meant.

Fresh Eye Technique
The idea behind the fresh eye technique is to provide a different perspective to a problem by having individuals who are not familiar with the problem give their observations and suggestions. The problem is first stated as clearly

as possible in written form and then presented to an individual or individuals who have little or no familiarity with the problem. Their suggestions are recorded and given to the value analysis team. The team then evaluates and discusses the various observations and suggestions for potential insight and problem-solving potential.[7]

Heuristic Ideation Technique (HIT)

The HIT provides a systematic procedure for exploring potential improvements to a given situation. First, a grid is developed consisting of various factors that are components of the problem. Next, all potential combinations are reviewed, with all combinations that currently exist or are impossible being crossed out. The remaining combinations are then numbered and evaluated for improvement potential. Last, the best two combinations are developed further. Williams, Lacy, and Smith use the example of food packaging. One axis of the grid might be packaging format, such as can, aerosol, jar, bag, box, or tube, and the other axis might be food type, such as bread, chips, juice, vegetables.[8] All combinations of packaging and food type that currently exist are crossed out as are combinations that are not feasible, such as aerosol and bread. The remaining combinations are then numbered and evaluated.

Forced Fit Relationship Technique

This approach takes two unrelated concepts and relates them to explore potential solutions. One of the concepts relates to the problem under investigation while the second is totally unrelated. For each concept, generate a list of 10 to 20 attributes or characteristics. Next, take the first characteristic or attribute from the first concept's list and combine it with the first characteristic or attribute from the second concept's list. Repeat this step, combining each characteristic or attribute from the first list with each on the second list. This will generate from 100 to 400 combinations. Use each new combination as a stimulus to generate new ideas. This process forces the participants to break through traditional approaches by generating completely unrelated patterns that can stimulate new solutions.[9]

---

[7]Alvin J. Williams, Steve Lacy, and William C. Smith, "Purchasing's Role in Value Analysis: Lessons from Creative Problem Solving," *International Journal of Purchasing and Materials Management* 28 (2) (Spring 1992), p. 40.

[8]Williams, Lacy, and Smith, pp. 40–41.

[9]Williams, Lacy, and Smith, p. 41.

Suppliers

Suppliers are potentially rich sources of ideas. They can be asked to suggest design or specification changes that would reduce manufacturing cost. Suppliers can also be asked to observe the use of their product by the buying firm to ensure proper use and potentially generate product improvements that will reduce costs of either manufacturing or quality. Programs for supplier involvement may be formal, such as supplier workshops, or informal requests of suppliers. It may even be desirable to include a supplier representative on a particular value analysis team. The buyer must be aware of potential ethical issues, such as having one supplier be involved in the value analysis of another's product or asking a supplier to bid on another supplier's value analysis ideas.

It should be noted here there are many other value analysis techniques, such as functional comparison; blast, create, refine; roadblock identification; functional analysis system; and use of industry specialists. The superior results of value analysis are achieved because of the multidisciplinary approach coupled with the systematic application of the techniques.

SURPLUS AND DISPOSAL ACTIVITIES

Surplus and disposal activities are a common responsibility of the purchasing function. A 1988 Center for Advanced Purchasing Studies (CAPS) study reports that 57 percent of the respondents indicated that they had responsibility for scrap and surplus disposal.[10] This is reinforced in the CAPS Purchasing Performance Benchmark reports for various industries, with the range of firms within an industry indicating responsibility for disposal of assets varying from 10 to 83 percent depending on the industry. Purchasing has this responsibility for several reasons. First, since purchasing is the major interface between users within the organization and suppliers, it has the greatest probability of knowing which items will need to be disposed of and what the needs of suppliers and users may be. Second, purchasing generally has the greatest knowledge of the markets in terms of potential customers and current market prices. Last, in a preventive mode, purchasing can alert users to potential disposal problems at a later

---

[10]Harold E. Fearon, *Purchasing Organizational Relationships* (Tempe, Ariz.: Center for Advanced Purchasing Studies/National Association of Purchasing Management, 1988), p. 14.

date and be alert to purchase requisitions that may have potential for creating excess inventory.

Disposal activities have received increased attention in recent years due to a variety of factors. With the ongoing concern about inventory levels, organizations are making a concerted effort to dispose of excess and obsolete stock, preferably with revenue or tax credits to offset the potential losses. Similarly, disposal of excess equipment or materials frees valuable facility space for future growth or reduces the firm's space requirements. Obsolescence, both technical and economic, has also contributed to the increased disposal activity. With the short product life in many industries due to technical change, product modifications may cause parts to be obsolete in a matter of months. The effects of obsolescence can be ameliorated somewhat by a standardization program.

Classes of Goods

Disposal activities cover a wide range of materials and equipment from inventory to hazardous materials. Categories are inventory, equipment, scrap, waste, and trash.

Inventory
Inventory items may require disposal because they are in excess of anticipated requirements or obsolete. Excess or surplus inventories may be caused by factors such as optimistic sales forecasts, over ordering, or sudden changes in market conditions. Obsolete inventories may be caused by poor planning of a design change or sudden design changes necessitated by product performance problems or competitor actions.

Equipment
Equipment may be either surplus or obsolete. Surplus or excess equipment is equipment that is still serviceable but is no longer needed. This could be due to a replacement or change in the process that no longer requires the old equipment. For example, in a university it is not uncommon for a department to replace a file cabinet with a newer or larger model. The old file cabinet is declared excess and made available to other departments in the university. Equipment may be declared obsolete due to a process change, a change in technology, or because it is advantageous to replace it with newer equipment for cost reasons.

Scrap and Waste

Scrap is material that is the planned residue from normal operations. Scrap may also apply to equipment or tooling that is no longer serviceable and can only be disposed of as material. Classes of scrap include paper, paperboard, wood, ferrous metals, nonferrous metals, plastics, wood, glass, petroleum, and petroleum products. Waste is material that is unnecessary scrap, such as materials damaged by mishandling, improper setup techniques, and poor planning.

Trash

Trash is operational residue that has little or no market value. Basically, it includes any items that cannot be converted to scrap or made use of in some form or fashion.

Methods of Disposal

Materials or equipment can be disposed of in a variety of ways, such as through use, return, sale, donation, abandonment, recycling, or disposal of trash in a landfill or through burning. A brief discussion of each approach follows.

Use

The preferred way to dispose of any asset is to use it some way. The first step is to determine if any other area of the organization can use the material or equipment in its current condition. This can be accomplished by circulating a memo or putting the information in regular company internal publications. Since purchasing is in the position to best know the needs of other areas of the company, they can identify potential users of the material or equipment. Another way to use materials is to cannibalize all usable parts or components from excess or obsolete goods before disposing of the items by some other means.

Return

Excess or obsolete materials may be returned to the supplier for credit or a refund. A common practice of many suppliers is to charge a restocking fee for the materials returned. The willingness of a supplier to take back unused material will depend upon its age, current market for the product, and the volume of business it does with the buying firm. Returns to suppliers can yield 50 to 90 percent of item value.[11]

Sale

Excess or obsolete material and equipment or scrap may be sold through a variety of means such as company stores, advertisements, equipment brokers, recycling centers, or auctions. These can be profitable ways to dispose of materials and equipment. Sale to a dealer of surplus typically yields 10 to 40 percent of the original cost of salvaged items.[12] For example, Tektronix, Inc., an electronics firm, is able to realize revenues of around $80,000 per year on recycled paper and paperboard. This practice also saves the company about $220,000 in disposal fees.

Donation

Donating both inventory and equipment to approved organizations for a tax deduction is an approach that will not generate revenue but will reduce taxable income. For example, some Hewlett Packard branches donate used furniture and office supplies to local school districts and other non-profit agencies as tax-deductible contributions.[13]

Abandonment

An extreme approach is to leave the material or equipment in place and simply "walk away." This is not a desirable action, as the firm may still be liable for the removal and/or disposal of the items.

Recycling

Recycling of materials for reuse is a major focus in today's society. What is waste or by-product for one firm may be usable material for another. Some equipment may be sold as only scrap material, but at least it will be reused. For example, Intel has installed recycling equipment in order to reuse some of its chemicals.[14] Recycling can save as much as 50 percent of the money now spent for disposal and landfill charges.[15] For more information on recycling programs, contact:

---

[11]Richard A. Toelle and Richard J. Tersine, "Excess Inventory: Financial Asset or Operational Liability?" *Production and Inventory Management Journal,* Fourth Quarter 1989, p. 34.

[12]Toelle and Tersine, p. 34.

[13]Jennifer D'Alessandro, "Score Profits, Boost Image: Give Recyclables a Shot," *Electronic Buyers' News,* March 4, 1991, p. P6.

[14]D'Alessandro, p. P6.

National Recycling Coalition
1101 30th Street, NW, Suite 305
Washington, D.C. 20007
Phone: 202-625-6406

Disposal of Trash

If the material cannot be used, sold, returned, donated, or recycled, it will need to be disposed of in some form. That can range from simple disposal by burning, preferably for needed heat or power, to disposal in a land fill, or to use of hazardous material disposal sites. For hazardous materials, the handling and disposal costs are roughly eight times the original purchase price.[16] For example, the common solvent acetone sells for around $10 to $20 per gallon, yet disposal can cost over $200 per gallon. If you spill it on the ground, the cleanup costs $2,500 to $10,000 a gallon. If you spill it and do not clean it up, and if you are caught, the cost escalates to $200,000 to $1 million for cleanup, fines, and litigation.[17]

Legal and Regulatory Issues

When disposing of excess or obsolete materials or equipment there may be issues regarding warranties and liabilities as well as regulatory requirements that have to be addressed. The sale of items, goods, or equipment may result in implied warranties, such as merchantability and fitness for use, unless they are specifically disclaimed. If goods are sold as scrap or surplus, they should be specifically identified as such to avoid future problems.

The organization disposing of materials must be concerned about potential liability for its actions. Clear disclaimers on goods and equipment sold or donated will reduce the organization's potential liability. This is why abandonment is not a desirable strategy. Liability for hazardous materials follows ownership; that is, if an organization ever had ownership of a

---

[15]Patricia C. Bayers and Dona S. Cook, "Recycling Trash into Dollars: How to Overcome Objections to Recycling," *From Revolution to Evolution: The Next 75 Years,* Proceedings of the 75th Annual International Purchasing Conference (Tempe, Ariz.: National Association of Purchasing Management, 1990), p. 181.

[16]Michael E. Heberling, "Environmental Purchasing: Separating the Emotions from the Facts," Presentation at the 78th International Purchasing Conference, San Antonio, Tex., May 1993.

[17]Richard Schickling, "It's Easy Being Green," *Electronic Buyers' News,* August 3, 1992, p. 41.

hazardous material, that orgnization will have liability for its disposal. Even turning the material over to an authorized disposal firm will not relieve the firm's potential liability until the material involved is no longer a hazardous substance. Even disposal through legal and appropriate means today may result in a future liability if the practice becomes illegal in the future. The disposal of materials is governed by the Resource Conservation and Recovery Act of 1976.

PURCHASING'S ROLE

The topics covered in this chapter are generally referred to as ancillary supply functions because they do not fit into the standard supply process. Yet purchasing has a major responsibility for these areas since it has a responsibility to seek the maximum value for each product or service it procures. It is the buyer's responsibility to challenge wasteful and avoidable costs. Purchasing must consider the total cost of an item, not just the purchase price. For example, some suppliers of hazardous materials now offer to take back and dispose of the residual hazardous by-products. Clearly, this package will be more expensive than the simple purchase.

Purchasing also has a responsibility to investigate new materials and supplies that may lower the total cost of use. For example, a company may want to replace a relatively low purchase cost solvent that requires special disposal with a slightly higher cost solvent that does not require special disposal treatment.

Purchasers become aware of what makes some products more expensive than others and what features increase costs. Purchasing is in a strategic position to evaluate each requirement and specification as it must pass purchasing's review. Purchasing, therefore, is the most logical place to originate cost reduction activities.

CHAPTER SUMMARY

This chapter has focused on a variety of techniques aimed at lowering the costs of supply. The key points are:

- Standardization can be government specified, industry based, or company specific and can be for a product, service, or process.

- Standardization benefits include inventory reduction, lower prices through increased volumes, decreased control costs, and shorter new product introduction times.
- The steps for developing a standardization program are identification of potential areas for improvement, formation of a team or committee, data collection, generation of an improvement proposal, proposal implementation, and program follow-up.
- Cost reduction and avoidance programs include organization-wide buying agreements, such as centralized buying, lead division buying, and commodity councils; cooperative or pooled purchasing; long-term agreements; and total requirements contracting.
- Value analysis and value engineering provide a formal process for attaining the best product value to accomplish the required function at the lowest possible total cost.
- The steps in the value analysis process are identification, appraisal, solution generation, solution evaluation, implementation planning and execution, and project follow-up.
- Techniques that are useful in the value analysis/engineering process include checklists, brainstorming, functional cost analysis, the fresh eye technique, the heuristic ideation technique, the forced fit relationship technique, and the use of suppliers.
- Classes of goods for disposal include inventory, equipment, scrap and waste, and trash.
- Methods of disposal of materials or equipment include use, return, sale, donation, abandonment, recycling, or disposal in a landfill.
- The disposal of materials or equipment may raise legal issues regarding warranties, express or implied, and liability, especially regarding hazardous materials.
- Purchasing plays a vital role in standardization and cost reduction because of its strategic place in the supply process.

REFERENCES

Cavinato, Joseph L. *Purchasing and Materials Management.* St. Paul, Minn.: West Publishing Company, 1984.

Dobler, Don W., David N. Burt, and Lamar Lee, Jr. *Purchasing and Materials Management,* 5th ed. New York: McGraw-Hill Publishing Company, 1990.

Heinritz, Stuart, Paul V. Farrell, Larry Giunipero, and Michael Kolchin. *Purchasing: Principles and Applications,* 8th ed. Englewood Cliffs, N.J.: Prentice Hall, 1991.

Miles, Lawrence D. *Techniques of Value Analysis and Engineering,* 2nd ed. New York: McGraw-Hill Book Company, 1972.

CHAPTER 7

MANAGING THE SUPPLY BASE

INTRODUCTION

Bethlehem Steel's Burns Harbor plant has set up an MRO buying plan based on a single-sourced, bin-stocking concept. The concept is estimated to have saved Burns Harbor more than $29 million since 1984. Burns Harbor uses 21 "supplier agreements" which account for approximately 80 percent of MRO purchases. Each supplier of a particular commodity supplies all products used by the Burns Harbor plant in that product line. Pricing is on a "cost plus" basis with a profit margin agreed upon for every product. Bethlehem estimates that the average price of materials is five to ten percent lower than before.[1]

Managing the supply base is a major concern in purchasing today. The goals of managing the supply base are driven by the objectives of purchasing, such as quality, delivery, quantity, price, and service. Recent Center for Advanced Purchasing Studies (CAPS) Purchasing Performance Benchmarks have shown the average number of suppliers per firm to range between 750 and 20,000, with most firms in the 2,000 to 7,000 range. This is in sharp contrast to companies like Xerox, who cut their supply base by 4,700 suppliers in one year to 400 suppliers, and Apple, with 400 suppliers worldwide.[2] Suppliers are now viewed as critical to a firm's success.

This chapter will first look at some of the issues leading to the current trend toward integrating suppliers into the firm, including current general sourcing strategies. Next, the arguments for reducing the supply base

---

[1]Jean M. Graham, "A Simple Idea Saves $8 Million a Year," *Purchasing,* May 21, 1992, pp. 47–48.

[2]National Center for Manufacturing Sciences, *Competing in World-class Manufacturing: America's 21st Century Challenge* (Homewood, Ill.: Business One Irwin, 1990), p. 216.

will be reviewed followed by a look at three methods for improving supplier performance. The three phases in the supplier certification process are presented followed by a review of the consequences for purchasing.

INTEGRATING SUPPLIERS

Traditionally, supply base management focused on evaluating suppliers, developing new sources, developing minority suppliers, and determining the appropriate number of suppliers. Purchasing policy favored the use of two or three suppliers for critical items. Having multiple suppliers protected the firm against interruptions in supply caused by strikes, political problems, or acts of God. Single sourcing was to be tolerated if the quantities to be purchased were small or if suppliers held critical patents, offered lower freight rates, gave exceptional discounts, or agreed to carry the buyer's inventory (stockless purchasing).[3]

Multiple suppliers were also supposed to encourage price competition, thus ensuring that the firm received the lowest price available. The smaller supplier was stimulated to want a greater share of the business and therefore motivated to keep pushing the larger supplier. "Active competition thus stimulates both suppliers to vigorous performance."[4] This resulted in an emphasis on price, not a strategic relationship, and the total cost was ignored. "Pertinent supplier performance indices such as quality, delivery, reliability, and account servicing were sacrificed to the emphasis of purchasing costs."[5]

What has changed to cause purchasing professionals to rethink how to manage the supply base? First is the realization that firms are competing in a global marketplace. Previously a firm could compete on a variety of factors such as features, terms, and delivery, even if it was not recognized as the quality leader in an industry. Today, pressure from global competitors has driven organizations to the realization that they need to be cost and quality competitive to survive; therefore, the supply base must be supportive of those same goals.

---

[3]Donald W. Dobler, Lamar Lee Jr., and David N. Burt, *Purchasing and Materials Management,* 4th ed. (New York: McGraw-Hill Book Company, 1984), p. 98.

[4]Dobler, Lee, and Burt, p. 99.

[5]Michael J. Kierdorf, "Supplier Relationships in the 1990s," *From Revolution to Evolution: The Next 75 Years,* Proceedings of the 75th Annual International Purchasing Conference (Tempe, Ariz.: National Association of Purchasing Management, 1990), p. 25.

This global focus has led to increased competitiveness, not only in quality and cost, but also in lead times for new product introduction. Western firms rarely involved suppliers in the design process. The supplier normally saw a component after it had been designed and purchasing wanted a price and a delivery date. The traditional new product introduction time for an automobile was five years, with supplier involvement taking place about 18 months before manufacturing was scheduled to begin. Chrysler, through early supplier involvement strategies, was able to reduce its new product introduction time to three years for the Viper and 39 months for the LH series.[6]

Faced with these pressures, U.S. firms have come to the realization that the supply base affects the organization's ability to compete. Suppliers can offer knowledge and ideas for product innovation beyond the capabilities and resources of the buying company. According to a survey by Clark, "Supplier involvement (and strong supplier relationships) accounts for about one-third of the man-hours advantage and contributes four to five months of the lead-time advantage [held by Japanese automakers]."[7] Additionally, improving supplier relations leads to improved efficiency. Integrating the suppliers into the operations of the firm leads to lower inventories, faster overall response times, higher quality, and lower total costs. Also, positive supplier relationships provide a foundation for continued growth and responsiveness to competitive demands. Without these relationships, firms will have "less and less ability to respond to improving performance standards of manufacturing industries, endure market fluctuations, reduce costs of inventory and delivery, and prevent quality problems caused by the sources. It's a matter of long-term survival."[8]

What are the implications for managing the supply base? First, firms need to view suppliers as an integral part of a supply process. This leads to developing meaningful relationships with suppliers. The adversarial relationship between buyer and supplier must be dissolved. It is difficult, if not impossible, to develop solid relationships with thousands of suppliers; thus one must reduce the supply base. Second, as buyer-supplier relationships

---

[6]Ernest Raia, "Design 2000: LH Story," *Purchasing,* February 18, 1993, p. 55.

[7]Kim B. Clark, "Project Scope and Project Performance: The Effect of Parts Strategy and Supplier Involvement on Product Development," *Management Science* 35 (October 1989), pp. 1247–63.

[8]Harold J. Steudel and Paul Desruelle, *Manufacturing in the Nineties: How to Become a Mean, Lean, World-Class Competitor* (New York: Van Nostrand Reinhold, 1992), pp. 345–346.

are developed, they will lead to long-term purchasing and supply commitments. However, a long-term supply commitment is more than a long-term contract, which is still a one-way oriented document. Whereas a contract normally has a specified time period with well-defined conditions and terms, a supply commitment is more fluid, focusing on maintaining the relationship. Third, this increased interaction between buyer and seller requires improved communications. Counterparts within the buying and supplying organizations need to be able to interact with each other regularly to facilitate the solution of problems. Fourth, the improved relationships lead to early supplier involvement in new product design, improving the manufacturability and reducing the costs of current products.

Sourcing Strategies

Managing the supply base is taking on new meaning in today's globally competitive markets. Purchasing professionals are receiving new pressure to ensure delivery, quality, quantity, and service while reducing price. Many sourcing strategies are being used today to meet these objectives. Sourcing strategies can be categorized into four approaches: outsourcing, quality improvement, supply continuity, and service improvement.

Outsourcing
Outsourcing is the current version of make versus buy. Whereas the make versus buy decision is usually oriented toward one component or part, the outsourcing decision may include a whole subassembly. For example, in manufacturing the LH series automobiles, Chrysler outsourced the entire rear suspension module to A. O. Smith.

Another form of outsourcing is the use of original equipment manufacturers (OEMs) as suppliers. The OEM produces the entire product and puts on the product the name or logo of the customer, who then sells the product as its own. An example is the original IBM graphics printer that was made by Epson for IBM. The rationale for this approach is that the supplier has greater expertise than the buyer. This reduces the need for the buyer to have facilities dedicated to a particular product line, thus giving the buyer greater flexibility.

Quality Improvement
Quality improvement strategies are aimed at improving the quality of materials and components that arrive from the supplier. One approach has

been the development of supplier quality programs. These programs are usually aimed at measuring the supplier's quality, possibly using statistical process control (SPC) techniques, and working with the supplier to improve its quality. Another approach is the use of supplier certification programs. Supplier certification can take many forms, but the most common focus is on quality. The desired outcome of a supplier certification program is to be able to move materials directly from the supplier to the production process, where they can be used immediately.

Supply Continuity

Supply continuity strategies include long-term contracts, partnerships, ownership interest, and vertical integration. One strategy is to use long-term contracts. The CAPS Purchasing Performance Benchmarks reports for several industries show that the percentage of purchases bought on long-term contracts ranges between 15 and 36 percent. A firm may enter into long-term contracts or supplier certification without entering into a partnering arrangement. The development of a partnership arrangement implies developing a two-way relationship. Another, although less often used approach, is to purchase an interest in a supplier to gain continuity of supply. An example is the purchase of a 20-percent interest in Intel by IBM. An even rarer approach these days is backward vertical integration, the outright purchase of a supplier to ensure supply. Most firms today would favor the "virtual integration" approach of Apple, where the relationships with suppliers are so close that, to the outsider, suppliers appear as subsidiaries.

Service Improvement

A fourth set of strategies focuses on improving supplier service. A major strategy today is early supplier involvement. This involves getting suppliers into the design process to reduce the cost of manufacture. Another strategy buyers are taking is improving the supplier's inventory service level through consignment programs, supplier stocking (also called breadman programs), and supplier maintenance of minimum inventories. All three are aimed at reducing the firm's cost of owning and managing inventory.

Other Sourcing Issues

There are two other issues relevant to developing a sourcing strategy. The first is the choice of domestic versus international suppliers. There are many arguments in favor of each choice. From a sourcing strategy viewpoint, the use of domestic suppliers may be preferred, since it should shorten the supply chain and make communication easier. However, international suppliers may have technology and/or cost advantages and be better able to service the firm's needs worldwide. The second issue is the development of minority, women-owned, and small business suppliers. The natural result of supplier consolidation strategies may be the reduction in the number of minority, women-owned, and small business suppliers the firm uses. It will take a conscious effort on the part of management as well as purchasing to ensure that the use of minority suppliers is a part of the organization's sourcing strategy.

SUPPLIER REDUCTION STRATEGIES

The controversy over single versus multiple sourcing continues to rage. The answer to this controversy is dependent upon the strategic role the supply base plays in helping the firm compete. Chrysler consciously chose to single source major components of its new LH series automobiles with astounding results. Chrysler recruited about 200 suppliers as compared to the usual 600 to 700 without a single bid.[9] The results of developing a sourcing strategy for every major component were that the entire project was completed in about 39 months, with the finished product below weight and cost targets compared to the traditional five-year design cycle. Lubben states the case against multiple sourcing eloquently:

> Improving efficiency, therefore, starts with weaning management from traditional purchasing policies and practices that require solicitation of multiple bids (multiple quoting), short-term contracts, and "second sourcing." These practices consume much time and result in extensive housekeeping activities such as supplier visits, material tracking, expediting, and returning defective material. Making better use of buyer time is achieved by devoting more time toward planning and implementing improvement programs.[10]

The other major argument for multiple sourcing is lower prices, which should result from having suppliers compete for the business through competitive bidding. Lubben responds with:

---

[9]Donald F. Wood and James C. Johnson, Contemporary Transportation, 4th ed. (New York: Macmillan Publishing Company, 1993), p. 56.

[10]Richard T. Lubben, *Just-In-Time Manufacturing* (New York: McGraw-Hill Book Company, 1988), p. 205.

Multiple price quotations give management confidence that the lowest price was obtained. This outdated process is inefficient primarily because multiple quoting is usually directed at obtaining the lowest prices for a product, not necessarily the best balance of quality and price.[11]

The case for single sourcing is based less on cost issues and more on management issues. Beyond the traditional rationale for single sourcing discussed previously, a single source makes the coordination of production schedules easier, develops a sense of obligation and responsibility in the supplier, and improves the buyer's position for negotiating price discounts because of larger volumes. Also, the resulting higher volumes make frequent deliveries more practical, as does the ability to supply several different items in one shipment. The supplier monitoring and performance evaluation process is also simplified with fewer suppliers to manage, resulting in lower administrative costs.

METHODS TO IMPROVE SUPPLIER PERFORMANCE

Three approaches to improving supplier performance are improved communication, early supplier involvement, and supplier evaluation. This section will look at these three topics.

Communication

One of the major ways to improve supplier performance is improved communication. For example, Hewlett Packard discovered that there were major discrepancies in their suppliers' understanding of the date on the purchase order. An amazing 60 percent of the time the buyers and suppliers were not clear about what they had agreed upon. Changing the purchase order to make the information more clear was one of the major ways on-time deliveries were improved by 30 percent where on-time delivery was defined as between three days early to zero days late.[12]

How can a firm improve communication? One way is to make one or two individuals primarily responsible for all communication that takes place between the firm and the supplier. Having these individuals involved

---

[11]Lubben, p. 205.

[12]National Center for Manufacturing Sciences, p. 220–21.

in every exchange between the two companies ensures that there is consistency of message over time. The downside of this approach is that it may slow down the communication process if every communication has to pass through one or two individuals. The analogy is the difference between one lane in each direction on a road and four lanes in each direction. More traffic can flow through four lanes than through one, speeding the flow, but there is little coordination across lanes.

A second approach is to facilitate supplier involvement. Several methods include supplier conferences, symposia, and workshops. Supplier conferences can be used to provide a forum to present new information to suppliers about new products or new programs such as supplier certification. They are useful in passing on general information but are not conducive to building long-term relations. Supplier symposia bring a cross section of suppliers who are not competitors together in a problem-solving mode to deal with issues like packaging or shipping problems that are common to the group. These groups can meet on a monthly to quarterly basis, with rotating membership. Supplier workshops involve bringing to the buying firm a variety of people from one particular supplier to develop an awareness of the role its products and services play in the firm's business. Ideally they should not only observe the use of their product, but should actually have the opportunity to use or install it. For example, as Tennant was showing a supplier where its product was assembled, the supplier pointed out that Tennant was incorrectly using a vise to hold the parts in place, causing the parts to distort, and thereby creating a quality problem.[13]

Early Supplier Involvement

Early supplier involvement (ESI) is the process of getting suppliers involved in product development. Bringing suppliers into the design process creates opportunities to reduce cost, improve quality, and shorten development time. For example, the use of suppliers in the design of the IBM ProPrinter cut the development time by 40 percent, bringing the product to market two months earlier than projected while meeting cost targets. Bringing purchasing and suppliers together in the design process helps avoid many potential problems such as over specification, improves

---

[13]Roger L. Hale, Ronald E. Kowal, Donald D. Carlton, and Tim K. Sehnert, *Made in the USA* (Minneapolis, Minn.: Tennant Company, 1991), p. 125.

product standardization, and reduces communication problems. Involving suppliers and purchasing in new product discussions from the beginning enables specifications to be developed jointly. This eliminates the traditional cycle of design, quote, redesign, requote, etc. Thus purchasing and suppliers don't have to become involved after the engineers are finished without knowing what events have already transpired and what the issues were in the original design. Early supplier involvement is very difficult, if not impossible, to undertake with multiple sourcing, because suppliers may not be motivated to expend time and resources at the design stage with no guarantee of receiving the business later. Additionally, there could be potential antitrust issues with competitors working together to provide a product for the buying firm.

Measuring Supplier Performance

If one believes the adage, "You get what you measure," then how a firm evaluates its suppliers' performance becomes a key tool in improving performance. The criteria used for evaluating supplier performance generally fall into several categories: quality, delivery, cost/price, service, and managerial. The specific measures used within a category will vary from firm to firm and will depend upon the performance measures used for supplier certification. In a survey by Raedels and Buddress, buyers ranked the categories in the following order: delivery, quality, cost/price, and service.[14] These rankings are consistent with the percent of firms indicating that they use each criterion for evaluating supplier performance in CAPS Purchasing Performance Benchmarking studies of the telecommunications services and the telecommunications equipment industries.

Quality measures may include incoming defect rate, product variability, and number of customer complaints. Additional measures might include supplier's quality philosophy, use of statistical process control, and documented process capabilities.

---

[14]Alan R. Raedels and Leland Buddress, "A Preliminary Comparison of Purchasing Performance Measures with Customer and Supplier Performance Measures," *Developments in Purchasing and Materials Management,* Proceedings of the 1993 National Association of Purchasing Management Annual Academic Conference (Tempe, Ariz.: National Association of Purchasing Management, 1993), pp. 58–63.

Delivery measures could include on-time delivery percentage, availability of product within quoted lead time, and quantity accuracy. Secondary measures might include current lead time estimates and ability to respond inside quoted lead time.

Service measures might include length of time required to settle claims and invoice accuracy. Additional measures could include availability of a supply plan, willingness to be involved in the design process, availability of a stocking program, engineering support, and quality of representatives (sales, customer service, and technical).

Cost/price measures could include product cost, price reductions, and cost of transportation. Other measures may include worldwide competitiveness, willingness to participate in price reviews, and minimum buy requirements.

Managerial measures include management commitment to quality and partnering, labor relations, employee turnover, level of management ownership, and similarity of values and beliefs.

SUPPLIER CERTIFICATION

In the process of reducing the supply base, many firms are using supplier certification as a means to select the suppliers who will be reliable over the long term. Many firms shy away from the term "partner," which has a legal connotation, and use preferred or certified supplier in its place. The purposes of certification are to (1) determine the suppliers with whom the firm should enter into long-term relationships, (2) improve quality and delivery reliability, and (3) provide a means for monitoring ongoing performance of a supplier. Generally, suppliers are sorted into one of several categories. Tennant Corporation uses three categories, qualified, conditionally qualified, and unqualified, while the James River Corporation uses four, qualified, preferred, certified, and unqualified. As firms move into supplier certification they need to remember that this is an ongoing process focused on improving the supply process and the buyer-supplier relationship.

Certification Process

There are three primary phases in the supplier certification process. First is qualifying suppliers to participate in the program; second is evaluating suppliers; and third is certifying and following up suppliers. Table 7.1 presents the steps for each of the three phases of the supplier certification process.

Qualifying Suppliers

The first step is the formation of the certification steering team. The steering team should be composed of representatives from at least purchasing, quality assurance, engineering, and production. The team will have the responsibility for developing the criteria to be used in the evaluation of suppliers and administering the certification process. The steering team also will have the responsibility for forming individual product/supplier teams that will work with the individual suppliers.

The second step in the process is the determination of certification criteria. Tables 7.2, 7.3, and 7.4 present the certification criteria of the Tennant Corporation, the James River Corporation, and a distributor evaluation system respectively. There is a fair amount of overlap between the various systems. The development of a set of criteria should include a review process by suppliers to ensure that the criteria are realistic and measurable.

Suppliers to participate in the certification process can be selected in several ways. One approach is to invite suppliers to a general session where the process is explained. Suppliers can then be asked to indicate if

TABLE 7.1
Steps in the Supplier Certification Process

Phase 1—Qualifying Suppliers

1. Form certification steering team
2. Determine certification criteria
3. Select suppliers to participate

Phase 2—Evaluating Suppliers

1. Form supplier evaluation teams
2. Evaluate suppliers
3. Review evaluation with supplier
4. Develop action plan with supplier

Phase 3—Certification and Follow-up

1. Evaluate outcomes of action plan
2. Award certification when criteria are met
3. Monitor performance

TABLE 7.2
Tennant Corporation Supplier Certification Criteria

1. On-site assessment
   Quality systems
   Organization
   Market analysis
   Financial analysis
   Operating systems
   Support capabilities
   Policies
   Manufacturing assessment

2. Management involvement
   Required involvement of supplier's top management

3. Mutual understanding of requirements
   Review "Supplier Requirements and Information Manual"

4. Supplier corrective action request systems
   Supplier must understand the process and respond within specified time
   frame

5. Reliability performance
   Ability to work with and meet reliability goals

6. Incoming lot performance
   Expectation of 12 months or 100 consecutive lots of 100 percent acceptance

7. Piece part performance
   Meet goal for number of defect-free parts based upon commodity type

8. Delivery performance
   Goal of 100 percent on-time delivery

Source: Roger L. Hale, Ronald E. Kowal, Donald D. Carlton, and Tim K. Sehnert, *Made in the USA* (Minneapolis, Minn.: Tennant Company, 1991)

TABLE 7.3
James River Supplier Certification Criteria

1. Quality
   Specifications developed around critical performance areas
   Complaint/problem history
   Processing consistency and resulting quality
   [Statistical quality control]-based quality data submitted
   Uses SPC and DOE techniques
   Process variability reductions per quality data submitted

Continued

Process capabilities documented which meet stated specifications
Formal, real quality philosophy
Uses quality improvement plans and teams
Partnership driven; will honor our confidentiality agreement

2. Service
Sales, customer service, and technical reps courteous, knowledgeable, and professional
Availability per lead time
Percent on-time deliveries
Plans of supply
Continuous improvements—inventories, paperwork, lead times
Documentation—acknowledgements, invoices, material data safety sheets, etc.
Prompt, fair claims settlement if they exist
Transportation
Order entry and tracking system
Storage facilities
Communications, flexibility, and responsiveness

3. Cost of Use
Supplier working with us in cost reduction/effectiveness efforts
Cost of purchase—price, freight, inventory, terms, etc.
Cost of processing—efficiency, throughput rates, waste, etc.
Cost of quality—claims, lost sales, complaints, etc.
Cost of service—early deliveries, late deliveries, excess handling, etc.

4. Design and Technology
Responsiveness—testing, information, samples
Sufficient testing
Technical communication
Problem analysis/trouble shooting capabilities
Knowledge and sensitivity to customer needs and applications
Innovation—timely introduction of new, improved products
Process control hardware

6. Values and Beliefs
Accuracy of information
Confidentiality
Win/win perspective
Similarity to James River's values and beliefs
Partnership driven
Safety
Housekeeping
Labor-management relations
People development

Scale: 1 = Not acceptable
2 = Marginal
3 = Acceptable
4 = Good
5 = Excellent

TABLE 7.4
Distributor Certification Criteria

---

1. Internal Operations—80 points
   Management quality leadership
   Extent of quality commitment
   Identification of quality control points in all processes
   Ability of employees at all levels to relate the tasks they perform to meeting
      customer needs

2. Continuing Process Improvement—100 points
   Specific results attributable to the quality process
   Documented improvements in methods and processes
   Future improvements documented and methods established to insure
      improvements will be implemented

3. Performance Measurement and Tracking—30 points
   Data collection to support measures such as on-time delivery, shipping dis-
      crepancies, invoice accuracy, line item fill rates.
   Performance indicators established for all partnering agreements

4. Problem Solving Capability—70 points
   Preventive action orientation rather than reactive response
   Problem solving performed in a timely and conclusive manner
   Employees at all levels must be involved in identifying and solving problems

5. Employee Participation and Involvement—100 points
   Active participation and involvement by all employees in the quality
      process
   Employees empowered to take action

6. Procedure Development—80 points
   Written procedures established for all processes
   Procedures consistently followed

7. Training—40 points
   Continuous quality training in place and operating

Source: William S. Wehr, "Selecting World Class Distributors: A Case Study," *The World Marketplace in 1992,* Proceedings of the 77th Annual International Purchasing Conference, Tempe, Ariz.: National Association of Purchasing Management, 1992. Used by permission.

they are interested in participating in the process. An alternate approach is to inform all current suppliers by letter about the process that will take place and indicate that the firm will be selecting suppliers to participate. The firm then approaches individual suppliers to participate based upon the current performance of the supplier and how that supplier fits into the long-range supply needs of the firm. The ideal suppliers to begin working with are the 10 to 20 percent of suppliers that account for most of a firm's purchases. The

CAPS Purchasing Performance Benchmarking studies show that any-where from 7 to 30 percent of a firm's suppliers account for 90 percent of the purchases, with an average of around 18 percent.

Evaluating Suppliers

Once suppliers are selected, the steering team forms a product/supplier team to perform the actual assessment. The composition of the team should be similar to the steering committee, with representatives from purchasing, engineering, production, and quality assurance who are associated and familiar with the product or product family for which the supplier is being considered. It would be desirable to have a similar set of representatives from the supplier to facilitate problem solving at subsequent stages.

The next step is to evaluate the suppliers. This usually involves a site visit that includes an inspection of the facility, review of the control sys-tems, interaction with engineering where appropriate, and talks with the supplier's management. Every member of the survey team has his or her own responsibilities, but the team should meet once or twice during the visit to compare notes and make sure all topics are covered. Upon return-ing home, the team develops a report covering all aspects of the criteria with recommendations for improvement.

The third step in the evaluation process is to review the evaluation with the supplier's representatives which should include top management as well as the functional representatives. Any discrepancies in the team's conclusions should be highlighted and addressed at that time. Fourth, the team should then work with the supplier to establish an action plan of what needs to be done for the supplier to achieve certification. The plan should have clearly identifiable activities with measurable outcomes.

Certification and Follow-up

At specified times, the evaluation team will assess the progress of the sup-plier toward achieving certification (Step 1—evaluate outcomes of action plan). One approach is to use intermediate classifications such as condition-ally qualified, initially qualified, or preferred to indicate the supplier's progress toward certification. The time frame for achieving certification will vary from supplier to supplier and can range from one to three years. For example, Tennant Corporation expects either 12 months or 100 consecutive lots without defect before a supplier can achieve qualified status.[15]

---

[15]Hale and others, p. 116.

When a supplier meets the certification criteria, a major award ceremony should be scheduled at the supplier's facility (Step 2). The award should be made by top management to the supplier's management. An appropriate plaque or other award that the supplier can display should be presented.

The final step in the process is the establishment of an ongoing monitoring program to ensure that the supplier remains in compliance. The program should include monitoring ongoing parameters such as quality and delivery as well as taking annual reviews with full audits every two or three years. Major changes in the supplier's process or products may trigger an audit or reevaluation. Additionally, reoccurring quality problems, a major product failure, customer complaints, or frequent shortages of material may be grounds for reevaluation of the supplier.

Making the Relationship Work

Several problems can arise in the certification process. One is the firm's ability to evaluate the supplier's production processes. The buying firm may have little or no expertise in the supplier's process or business. This potentially allows the supplier to conceal deficiencies. There is no guarantee that the certification process will expose flaws in the supplier's operations or procedures. A second problem is getting the supplier to care about the purchasing company's certification. The supplier may have 30 or 40 other customers who want to perform audits, and other customers' recommendations may not be consistent with your firm's needs. A supplier who is ISO 9000 certified may not consider your company's certification of any additional value. Last, are suppliers asked to meet a standard the buying firm can't meet? A good test for certification criteria is to apply it to internal operations before using it with suppliers.

How does a firm interest a supplier in establishing a long-term relationship? Potential inducements include long-term contracts, stability for the supplier, technical assistance, and higher volumes. The single factor that seems to be most important in establishing relationships is the level of desire by the management of both companies to work with and establish long-term relationships. A common theme in the certification criteria shown in Tables 7.2 through 7.4 is the fit between supplier and buyer philosophies. In fact, many purchasers will select a firm with poorer quality but a willingness to work with the buying firm to improve over a supplier with higher quality who is not responsive to the buyer's needs.

Role of ISO 9000 and Other Third Party Awards

Should a firm perform its own certification or rely upon the certification programs of others? Other supplier evaluation systems commonly used as models include ISO 9000, the Malcolm Baldrige National Quality Award, Motorola's Six Sigma, Ford's Q1, Chrysler's SQA, General Motors' Targets for Excellence, and those used by Rockwell, Xerox, Kodak, and Honda. The argument for accepting the certification from another of the supplier's customers is that it reduces costs and provides comparable information. The argument against this practice is that another firm may not have the same needs or standards as your firm. The value of a preferred supplier is not based just on its quality but also on its ability to help the buying firm compete with lower costs and new technology in the future.

One of the reasons for the increased interest in ISO 9000 is that it provides a third party assessment of a supplier's processes. The downside is that the certification reflects only whether the firm is following its own documented processes, with little or no indication of the level of those processes.

There have been some attempts to develop standardized supplier evaluations by industry. The automotive, steel, chemical, semiconductor, and industrial distribution sectors have all begun attempts to develop guidelines for supplier evaluation.[16]

PURCHASING CONSEQUENCES

The benefits to purchasing of reducing the supplier base are many. First, reducing the number of suppliers will lead to a reduction in overall product variability. Since many items will have only one or at most two suppliers, the time required to determine the source of problems will be reduced. Second, closer involvement with suppliers will enable purchasing to better meet the needs of both its internal customers and the firm's customers. With a focus on the long term, purchasing can now focus its efforts on finding ways to improve product quality and lower product cost rather than spend all its time filling out paper work and seeking the lowest price supplier. Third, increased involvement of suppliers in the product design process will lead to greater competitiveness in quality, cost, and new product development lead time, thereby improving the firm's position in global markets.

---

[16]Anne Millen Porter, "Audits Under Fire," *Purchasing,* November 5, 1992, pp. 50–55.

The change in the purchasing-supplier relationship from adversarial to cooperative will bring changes in purchasing. For one thing, purchasing will find itself participating on more multifunctional teams dealing with a variety of issues such as supplier certification, new product design, and internal operations problem solving. This will necessitate purchasing developing greater skills in working in teams, applying the problem-solving process, and working with the customer as well as the supplier. The purchasing professional will continually have to balance the benefits of multiple sourcing and single sourcing. Most importantly, purchasing will need to be active in developing a supply strategy for all major commodities and components that will support the firm's competitive strategy.

CHAPTER SUMMARY

This chapter has examined the issues in managing the supply base, including the supplier certification process. Key points are:

- The increased global competitiveness in quality, cost, and lead time has forced firms to reevaluate the role the supply base plays in helping to remain competitive.
- The changes in supply management involve viewing suppliers as an extension of the firm, developing long-term relationships with suppliers, and getting suppliers more involved in product design and improving manufacturability.
- Sourcing strategies include outsourcing, quality improvement, supply continuity, and service improvement. Other sourcing issues include the evaluation of domestic versus international suppliers and the development and maintenance of minority, women-owned, and small business suppliers.
- Supplier reduction is based on the premise that it is easier and more cost effective to develop and manage a smaller rather than a larger supply base by using single sourcing where appropriate.
- Improving the communication with suppliers through a variety of means will improve the ability of the supplier to meet the firm's needs in a timely fashion.
- Early supplier involvement in the design process can pay large dividends in reducing product development time, improving product performance, and reducing product costs.

- The selection of appropriate measures of performance for supplier quality, delivery, service, cost/price, and managerial capability will go a long way toward improving supplier performance.
- The purposes of supplier certification are to determine with which suppliers to develop long-term relationships, to improve quality and delivery reliability, and to provide a means for monitoring ongoing performance.
- The certification process involves three major phases, qualifying the suppliers to participate in the program, evaluating suppliers, and certifying and following suppliers.
- The benefits to purchasing of reducing the supply base and improving supplier performance include reduced product variability, increased ability to meet both the internal and external customer's needs, and improved competitive position through better quality, lower costs, and reduced lead time.
- Purchasing professionals will need to improve their teamwork skills, realize that their relationships with suppliers are changing from adversarial to cooperative, and they will need to develop a supply strategy for each major material and component.

REFERENCES

Blackburn, Joseph D., ed. *Time-Based Competition: The Next Battleground in American Manufacturing.* Homewood, Ill.: Business One Irwin, 1991.

Burt, David N., and Michael F. Doyle. *The American Keiretsu: A Strategic Weapon for Global Competitiveness.* Homewood, Ill.: Business One Irwin, 1993.

Hale, Roger L., Ronald E. Kowal, Donald D. Carlton, and Tim K. Sehnert. *Made in the USA.* Minneapolis, Minn.: Tennant Company, 1991.

Heinritz, Stuart, Paul V. Farrell, Larry Giunipero, and Michael Kolchin. *Purchasing: Principles and Applications,* 8th ed.. Englewood Cliffs, N.J.: Prentice Hall, 1991.

Hutchins, Greg. *Purchasing Strategies for Total Quality.* Homewood, Ill.: Business One Irwin, 1992.

Leenders, Michiel, and David L. Blenkhorn. *Reverse Marketing: The New Buyer-Supplier Relationship.* New York: The Free Press, 1988.

Lubben, Richard T. *Just-In-Time Manufacturing.* New York: McGraw-Hill Book Company, 1988.

National Center for Manufacturing Sciences. *Competing in World-Class Manufacturing: America's 21st Century Challenge.* Homewood, Ill.: Business One Irwin, 1990.

Steudel, Harold J., and Paul Desruelle. *Manufacturing in the Nineties: How to Become a Mean, Lean, World-Class Competitor.* New York: Van Nostrand Reinhold, 1992.

Wehr, William S. "Selecting World Class Distributors: A Case Study," *The World Marketplace in 1992.* Proceedings of the 77th Annual International Purchasing Conference. Tempe, Ariz.: National Association of Purchasing Management, 1992.

THE FUTURE OF SUPPLY AND INVENTORY MANAGEMENT

CHAPTER 8

THE FUTURE OF SUPPLY AND INVENTORY MANAGEMENT

INTRODUCTION

In industries where competitiveness is more dependent on cost control of existing products than on rate of new product development, purchasing will need to be especially knowledgeable about the supplier's manufacturing process and capabilities. It will need to understand where and how component products are used. It will have to work with the people running the process in order to find standardization opportunities, whittle down the supply base, reduce inventories, and improve operating efficiency. In addition, more and more suppliers will be chosen by buying firms based on their capabilities and not quotations in some form of early sourcing process.[1]

As this quotation illustrates, major changes will be taking place in purchasing and materials management in the coming years. This final chapter will look to the future of purchasing's role in inventory management, logistics, ancillary supply functions, and supply management.

TRENDS IN INVENTORY MANAGEMENT

Several trends are evident in the area of inventory management. Perhaps the most important is the realization that inventories can best be managed by improving the supply process. Toward that end there will continue to be pressure to reduce inventories throughout the firm. This will result in a

---

[1]Robert M. Monczka and James P. Morgan, "Strategic Sourcing Management, Part 2," *Purchasing*, July 16, 1992, p. 65.

greater involvement by suppliers in managing inventories, more concern with reducing supplier lead times, and improvements in information transfer and accessibility.

Lower Inventories

With the increased attention to just-in-time (JIT) and total quality management (TQM) in businesses today, firms are extremely sensitive to inventory levels. A review of normal inventory behavior in economic upturns would show a rise in inventory levels. A look at the NAPM Report on Business Inventory Index over the last 10 years shows the index indicated growth in inventories only in approximately 12 of the 120 monthly periods in the manufacturing sector. Since inventory levels are dependent on the supply processes, purchasing will have increased responsibility for keeping raw material and component inventories as low as possible.

Supplier Involvement

An approach for reducing an organization's inventories that will receive more attention is supplier maintenance of the buying organization's inventories. One approach being used with greater frequency is the approach often used in grocery stores where the supplier maintains and stocks the inventory at the customer's facility. The benefit to the buying organization is that the supplier takes responsibility for controlling the inventory, thereby reducing the buying organization's control costs. Systems contracts will also continue to find new applications helping to reduce the buying organization's inventory levels.

Managing Lead Time

One of the prime reasons to maintain inventory is to deal with uncertainty of demand during lead time. Improving the production process will have minimal effect on reducing the total lead time. Total lead time includes product design, materials procurement, and manufacturing. A recent study by Robert Handfield reached the following conclusion:

> The impact on total lead time derived from reduced setups and smaller lot sizes appears to be minimal compared with the time lost because of poor supplier performance and poor designs. The most effective means a firm

can use to manage lead time is to develop sound relationships with its suppliers.[2]

The importance of lead time is reinforced by an article in *Purchasing* in which buyers indicated that they would rather pay a premium (as much as 19 percent) than wait six months for delivery of a machine tool and that a two-month delay was equated with a premium of 4 percent.[3]

Information

Several dimensions of the information flow will grow in importance. First, there will be continued growth of bar coding as a means of collecting information for inventory systems. This growth will occur because of two needs—(1) maintaining accurate inventory records as inventory levels are reduced, and (2) reducing the cost of obtaining the information. The continuing technological improvements and declining system costs will also contribute to the adoption of bar codes. Second, there will continue to be growth in the use of electronic data interchange (EDI) to improve information flow and shorten lead times. More organizations are understanding that the benefits of EDI extend beyond merely issuing purchase orders. This coupled with declining technology costs will cause EDI's adoption rate to increase. A third area is the importance of forecasting. Declining lead times and inventory levels will increase pressure on the materials organization to provide better forecasts of demand and usage. This is especially important for long lead time items to avoid stockouts without building inventories.

TRENDS IN LOGISTICS

Ongoing trends in logistics include the continued effects of deregulation, increased frequency of delivery as a result of the continuing adoption of just-in-time principles, and environmental pressures to reduce waste, especially from packaging materials.

---

[2]Robert B. Handfield, "The Role of Materials Management in Developing Time-Based Competition," *International Journal of Purchasing and Materials Management,* Winter 1993, p. 9.

[3]Ernest Raia, "JIT in the '90s: Zeroing in on Leadtimes," *Purchasing,* September 12, 1991, p. 57.

Deregulation

Deregulation will continue to affect purchasing. Buyers are just beginning to understand the potential benefits from deregulation, especially in motor freight. Previously, private carriers delivering materials to other divisions or finished product to customers were forced to return empty. Today, those backhauls can be filled with "for hire" shipments through the use of freight brokers. Conversely, buyers can reduce inbound costs by using someone else's backhaul capacity for inbound shipments.

Transportation providers are just beginning to understand the need to provide total system service including shipment tracking, consolidating, drop-shipping, and pickup in route. As the competition increases between and within transportation modes, the ability of carriers to provide these services will become critical for their success.

Frequent Deliveries versus Consolidation

Continuing watchfulness will be required for the tradeoff between the desire for frequent deliveries to keep inventories down and the potential for increased transportation and environmental costs of increased freight traffic, especially motor freight. Purchasing has the potential to help address this issue. One approach is the reduction of the organization's supply base so that larger quantities are coming from each supplier. The second is the consolidation of incoming shipments by ordering several different items from one supplier to create a truckload or carload shipment. Consolidation can also occur when orders from several suppliers in a region are combined into truckload or carload shipments. To accomplish consolidation, purchasing will need an information system that can provide the details of quantities, weight, points of origin, and due dates.

Packaging

The continuing pressures to reduce cost and waste will make packaging of inbound material a greater concern. The first priority will be the continued development and use of recyclable materials. A second will be trying to find ways to reduce the total amount of packaging. A third will be to reuse existing packaging, which creates some handling and transportation costs to return the packaging to the supplier. Finally, used packaging for which neither recycling nor alternate uses are possible must be environmentally friendly to facilitate disposal.

TRENDS IN ANCILLARY SUPPLY FUNCTIONS

As competitive pressures increase, organizations will turn more to the supply function to find ways to reduce costs. There will be increased concern about the disposal of surplus and waste equipment and materials and the related issues of recycling, hazardous materials, and green buying.

Continuous Improvement

Continuous improvement is now a permanent element of most operations. Since material cost is the major component of costs in many organizations, purchasing will need to place a high value on standardization, cost reduction, and value analysis. A recent study of the role of materials management in time-based competition indicated that industry leaders use a higher percentage of standard parts.[4] Value analysis and value engineering will continue to be valuable tools of cost reduction.

Investment Recovery

As resources continue to tighten, recovering funds from excess or obsolete materials and equipment will increase in importance. This is reflected in the change in terminology from scrap and surplus disposal to investment recovery. Purchasing's early involvement in product design decisions can help avoid using components that will be quickly outdated. Purchasing can also make arrangements with suppliers in advance for the handling of excess or obsolete materials and components.

Recycling

As disposal costs continue to rise, there will be an increased burden on purchasing to find ways to recycle materials to generate revenue and avoid major costs. Purchasing will need to have greater involvement in the selection of materials and supplies to ensure that consideration is given to recyclability. Organizations like Xerox and Chrysler are already beginning to consider the recycling requirements of the products they are designing today.

---

[4]Handfield, p. 5.

Hazardous Materials

With the number of materials designated hazardous already over 33,000, buyers will need to be cognizant of the packaging, transportation, and disposal requirements for hazardous materials. The current cradle-to-grave liability for hazardous materials means that the sourcing of disposal agents and carriers will be of prime importance to purchasing in the future.

Green Buying

The increasing concerns with disposal and recycling are leading to the concept of *green buying*. Green buying involves consideration of the total cost of the product including its generation, recyclability, disposal, and energy consumption.

TRENDS IN SUPPLY MANAGEMENT

A revolution is taking place in purchaser-supplier relations. There is a movement toward single source partnerships and reduction of the supply base. Other issues shaping this new relationship include multiple customer certifications and the adoption of Bose's JIT II concept.

Supplier Relations

As organizations understand the strategic advantages of a well-designed supply base, there will continue to be changes in supplier relations. There will be a continuation of the trends already under way of developing preferred suppliers, which leads to a reduction in the supply base. The key to shorter lead times, improved quality, and reduced costs lies with managing a smaller supply base. There will also be an increasing need for a supply base that provides flexibility not only to accommodate increases and decreases in demand but new product development as well. Early supplier involvement will be critical for reducing total lead time. This area is a prime candidate for increased purchasing involvement as evidenced by a recent survey by *Purchasing*, which identified coordination with manufacturing and design as one of several key areas where purchasing is missing opportunities to advance corporate strategy.[5]

Multiple Certification

Multiple certifications of suppliers by customers will continue to be a problem in the future. For example, one company spent 1,700 labor-hours hosting 37 visits from just three major customers over a 15-month period while another went through 40 different certification audits in one year's time.[6] Although ISO 9000 has the potential to address the problem, the ISO standard focuses primarily on the quality processes and not on other areas, such as product development or lead times. Several joint qualification consortia have been established to address this issue, such as the Joint Qualification Alliance (JQA), a consortium of Ford, Hewlett Packard, and AT&T Company; NMX, a consortium of AT&T's NCR unit, Motorola Inc., and Xerox Corporation; and the Computer Industry Quality Conference (CIQC), made up of computer manufacturers, Apple, Cray Research, Digital Equipment, Hewlett Packard, IBM, NCR, Sun, Tandem and Unisys. These consortia are having difficulty developing standards while avoiding antitrust issues. Some concern has been expressed as to whether the various consortia can effectively reduce the number of auditing standards. There is continued optimism that the consortia will be able to reduce the costs of certification to both supplier and purchaser.

JIT II®

JIT II is a registered service mark of the Bose Corporation. JIT II exists when a supplier's employee is located in the purchasing department of the customer, replacing the salesman and the buyer. This in-plant representative is empowered to use the customer's purchase orders to place orders with the supplying firm. The representative also participates in all meetings, both design and production, involving the supplying firm's product area and has complete access to customer facilities, personnel, and data. Benefits to the buying firm include

- freeing purchasing staff from administrative tasks;
- improved communication with the supplier;
- immediate and ongoing material cost reductions;

---

[5]Monczka and Morgan, p. 65.

[6]Paul Hyman and Jennifer D'Alessandro, "Customers Team Up to Build Standards," *Electronic Buyers' News,* January 3, 1994, p. P1.

- creation of supply standards; and
- providing a foundation for EDI.[7]

Benefits to the supplier include
- elimination of sales effort;
- increased volume of business;
- improved communication with the customer;
- no rebidding and no end date to the relationship;
- ability to sell directly to engineering; and
- effective invoicing and payment.[8]

Participation in the program is based on a supplier being judged best in a given commodity, providing superior quality and delivery performance and good cost levels, having acceptable engineering support, having an annual business volume exceeding $1 million, having a substantial number of purchase orders annually, and not being involved in trade secret or sensitive technologies.[9]

The concept is an interesting extension of partnerships. There are issues of control, responsibility, and whose interests are being furthered by the program. Although Bose treats the in-plant representative as it would its own buyer, requiring Bose sign-off on orders that exceed specified quantities or value, and all transactions are subject to audit, there are concerns about whose interests the representative serves on a day-to-day basis. When a conflict occurs between Bose's needs and the supplier's needs, how is it resolved? The concept has been used in several other companies but will probably catch on only in large companies for major commodities, products, or services. A prime candidate is transportation services, while items that require very little supplier involvement in design are not good candidates for the program.

CHAPTER SUMMARY

This final chapter has reviewed some of the key concepts developed in the text and looked to the future of purchasing's role in inventory manage-

---

[7]Anne Millen Porter, "'JIT II' Is Here," *Purchasing,* September 12, 1991, p. 62.

[8]Porter, p. 62.

[9]Porter, p. 64.

ment, logistics, ancillary supply functions, and supply management. Key points are:

- Trends in inventory management include continued pressure for lower inventories, more supplier involvement, more attention to managing supplier lead times, and improvements in information transfer and accessibility.
- Trends in logistics include continued effects of transportation deregulation, increased frequency of delivery as a result of the continuing adoption of just-in-time principles, and environmental pressures to reduce waste, especially from packaging materials.
- Trends in ancillary supply functions are driven by the need for ongoing cost reduction efforts. As a result there will be increased concern with the disposal of surplus and waste equipment and materials and the related issues of recycling, hazardous materials, and green buying.
- Trends in supply management include a movement toward single sourcing relationships, consolidation of the supply base, and the need for increased flexibility by both parties. Other issues shaping this new relationship include early supplier involvement in product design, multiple customer certifications, and the adoption of Bose's JIT II concept.

REFERENCES

Burt, David N., and Michael F. Doyle. *The American Keiretsu.* Homewood, Ill.: Business One Irwin, 1993.

Leenders, Michiel R., and Harold E. Fearon. *Purchasing and Materials Management,* 10th ed. Homewood, Ill.: Irwin, 1993.

INDEX

An n following a page number (as in 115n) refers to a footnote at the bottom of that page.

A

B